Raisin Cake

RAISINCAKE
Copyright 2009 by Rod Raymond
Be Your Own Personal Trainer Publications
227 Fairmont St.
Duluth, MN 55803
www.rodraymond.com
First Edition

All rights reserved. No part of this book
shall be reproduced, stored in a retrieval
system, or transmitted by any means
without written permission from the author.

International Standard Book Number:
978-0-9818250-8-3

Raisin Cake
LESSONS LEARNED FROM GRANDMA

BY ROD RAYMOND

Table of Contents

Grandma *07*
Raisin Cake. *11*
Grandma Lizabo's Raisin Cake *15*
Swallow the Frog *16*
Just Give *18*
Kids Need to be Kids *21*
Don't Swear *23*
Speak Clearly *24*
Some Things are Better Left Unsaid *26*
Sit Up *29*
Vital Posture Position *30*
Do It Right Now *35*
Know your Body *38*
Today is the Day *41*
Don't Stay a Beginner *43*
Live a Renaissance Life! *46*
Keep Heading North *49*

Travel When You're Young 55

Go Fishin' Often 61

Love Animals like Brothers and Sisters 64

Never go to a Social Event on an Empty Stomach . . . 67

Meet Someone New Every Day 68

Put People Before Money 71

Don't Stir the Poop 76

Don't Be an Outhouse, Flush it Away 78

Bury the Hatchet 80

If You Can't Eat it, Toss It! 86

Eat Your Vegetables 91

Grow a Garden 94

From Grandma's Pen 101

The Best Blankety-Blank Pickles 112

Elizabeth Lovold 1916-2006 114

Who are all the People in the Pictures? 117

Rod Would Like to Thank 121

Grandma

Grandma was born Elizabeth Lovold in 1916, in Beaver Bay, Minnesota. Her grandmother Elizabeth Slater, who was the area midwife, delivered her at home.

The tidbits of wisdom in this little book are about celebrating the beauty of life and dealing with the pains life also brings. In this crazy, upside-down, topsy-turvy world, turning to our elders sometimes can help us to slow down, taste the good things life has to offer, and make sense of its not-so-good-things.

Some of these insights are things Grandma told me directly. Some I learned by watching her. And some I have come to realize over time and can trace back to her gentle nature and quiet guidance. My guess is your grandma probably said, or still says, some of the same wise things to you.

Grandma had four daughters. She was adamant that they speak proper English and use proper manners. After supper they would sit, awestruck, as she told stories of her childhood.

I was probably 15 years old when I was finally allowed to sit at the grown-ups' table at Grandma's house. I can still hear her voice with that strong northern Minnesota accent, telling stories, sharing new plans and ideas. The feelings I would get while listening to her would take me high, and they would take me low. I never left her house the same boy I was when I arrived. Her Norwegian parables were filled with wisdom, humor, and common sense. She was not afraid to speak her mind, or the truth. Her optimism was seemingly never ending.

When her first grandson came along he couldn't say Elizabeth, so he called her Grandma Lizabo, and that was how we all knew her: as Grandma Lizabo.

She once told me, "Ya know, the guut news about turning 86 years old is that I can bring 85 years of my life experiences and stories into my 86th year. Not only that, but in 14 years I will get a letter from the President." Grandma Lizabo never made it to the elusive 100-year mark, but she did inject all of our lives with her good humor and optimism.

I wish every one of you could have enjoyed her story telling and great humor.

My hope is that the insights in this book can do for you what they have done for me. Grandma's wisdom gave me the confidence to live my best life. Because of her, I have adventure and spice in my daily walk. I have come to understand I am important, and I am meant to share my uniqueness on this planet. Grandma has helped me feel that I have endless love and connections with other people, the earth, and animals. She taught me the values and love that have helped sustain me.

And most of all, she taught me the need to give back.

So now I share Grandma's wisdom and wit with you.

Rod Raymond
Duluth, MN

Raisin Cake

I can't remember a time Grandma didn't have raisin cake in her fridge.

Whenever we visited, we'd have a piece of cake and a glass of milk. The cake was always moist and sweet, filled with plump raisins.

Although Grandma's raisin cake recipe is simple, her loving hands and dedication to its tradition made it a treasure. It filled Grandma's heart with joy to share this timeless treat with her friends, children, and grandchildren.

During World War II, Grandma and Grandpa moved to Two Harbors, Minnesota, where Grandma worked as a coal steamer in the shipyards while Grandpa sailed the Great Lakes as a merchant marine.

After the war they moved back to Beaver Bay, Minnesota, to run the Trading Post, a general store and bar. They sold groceries, sundries and, of course, sporting goods like fishing gear and hunting supplies.

On the cold, rugged shores of Lake Superior, there were few opportunities to meet other residents and share news. The Trading Post became one of those opportunities. A hot cup of coffee and a piece of raisin cake provided the perfect excuse to stop a while and catch up on all the latest news, or to simply spend a few moments in the company of others. To feel a connection.

Connection like that doesn't have to come from cake, or from any kind of food at all. It's the connection that happens when a handful of relatives or neighbors share some chit-chat or a story, and everyone's life is improved by speaking, listening, and being together.

Making and keeping connections requires three things: *An Idea, Dedication, and an Invitation.*

Grandma's raisin cake was about more than keeping a sweet treat around the house; it was a powerful idea that showed her dedication to an inviting home—to a level of love whose depth we may never understand.

For Grandma, baking raisin cake for her family and friends was one of many ways to express affection.

Grandma taught me:

Give what you love to do.

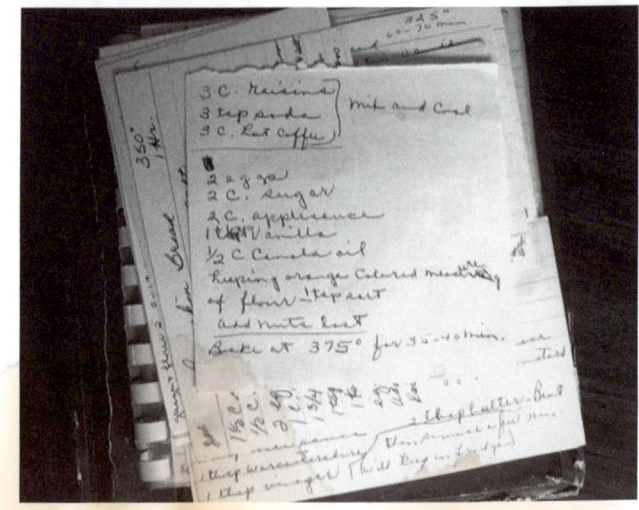

Grandma Lizabo's Raisin Cake

3 CUPS RAISINS
3 TSP SODA
3 CUPS HOT COFFEE
MIX AND COOL.

2 EGGS
2 CUPS SUGAR
2 CUPS APPLESAUCE
1 TSP VANILLA
1/2-CUP CANOLA OIL
3 HEAPING CUPS OF FLOUR
1 TSP SALT

ADD NUTS LAST.
BAKE AT 375 FOR 30 - 40 MINUTES.

Unfortunately for us, Grandma's secret for assembling those ingredients remains with her. Try your own version.

Swallow the Frog

If you're going to commit to something, then commit!

As Grandma would say, "If you are going to swallow a frog, you might as well go ahead and do it now, cause he ain't gettin' any prettier."

Grandma's father, Oscar, a commercial fisherman, immigrated to Lake Superior's North Shore from Christiansund, Norway, as a young man. He met and married Lena Slater, who was the granddaughter of immigrants from Prussia. Grandma was the second child of five, having three brothers and one sister.

Grandma's people came over on a boat from the old country. Like thousands of other immigrants, they bought a one-way ticket to a place they had only heard about from others.

Imagine that: A one way ticket on a hope for a better life. They had no guarantee. *Just hope*.

Grandma quoted her grandpa as saying: "You can't have one foot on the boat, and one foot on the pier forever. You need to make a decision."

And that's exactly how Grandma lived. No matter how painful, boring, or fun a decision was, she would make it then own it.

She would say: "There is a certain peace of mind you feel when you make a decision – even if it's the wrong one!"

She was known for putting 100 percent of her energy into cooking, family, her great garden, and everything she set her mind to. I don't remember her doing anything halfway.

Grandma rarely made decisions in haste, or without an open mind. She always said big decisions need to be thought through, and you need to be willing to change your mind and actions if the decision was wrong.

Grandma taught me:

The average results of decisions made in haste surely won't equal success.

Just Give

Grandma's desire to share her gifts, skills, and wisdom with all was endless. She taught her girls to knit, crochet, and embroider. Her hand-knit socks and mittens were a favorite Christmas gift for all the generations.

Even though arthritis later halted her knitting, she never stopped giving.

As a matter of fact, Grandma never talked of giving; she just gave. She didn't need to be asked to do things, but if she were asked, she would always do more than was asked of her.

Grandma taught me:

If you are not happy, you are most likely not giving enough.

Kids Need to be Kids

Kids have a mission: to be kids. Grandma would say that kids are supposed to nag, irritate, be selfish, and drive adults crazy; it's in their job description. She would also say they are supposed to laugh, be creative, learn, and play.

But Grandma didn't have patience for inappropriate screwing around. She was a fan of kids being kids until it was time for them to grow up, both literally and figuratively. Grandma said, "The reasons they make the chairs so small in kindergarden is so they don't fit you when you're in 11th grade."

She was also concerned with the future of today's kids. She said, "With all the over-stimulation, sensationalized media, disconnect from family, texting, humanless emails, and fear, it would be a miracle if today's kids grow up to be productive and happy adults."

Her solution was simple: Parents must keep families together by leading kids with loving discipline, wise decisions, and healthy examples.

Grandma taught me:

Kids need to be kids, and parents need to be adults.

Don't Swear!

My friend Jimmy lived across the street.

His mom would yell and scream at him endlessly. She would swear at him for anything and everything. Eventually, he just didn't hear her anymore.

One day when he was coming over to my house to play, a delivery man was driving down the street and wasn't paying attention.

As the truck neared Jimmy, it became obvious he would be hit. His mother busted out of the house, screaming at Jimmy to "get off the damn road!" She shouted a lot of swear words other than "damn," too. He didn't pay any attention to her. After all, it was just his mom yelling and swearing, like she always did.

The truck nearly killed him.

To this day I try not to raise my voice or swear unless I have a real reason for doing it.

Grandma taught me:

If you are going to yell and swear, make damn sure you have a good reason!

Speak Clearly

When Grandma was a child she struggled with math and just could not understand fractions. When her father (who was Norwegian and spoke broken English) tried to teach her, she truly got the point.

"My father asked me, 'What vun apple plus vun apple was?' And I said 'two apples.' Then he asked me 'What vun tird plus vun tird was?' And after several rounds of not getting it, it finally just sprung to my mind. I finally got it, as he asked me again, 'Vut is vun tird plus vun tird?'

"And in my excitement I replied 'two turds!' Dat vuz da right answer, but da wrong vurd. I spent a week doing da dishes."

No matter what language you speak, communication can sometimes be tricky. Grandma has led me to understand that clear communication first involves clear understanding.

In his book, *The 7 Habits Of Highly Effective People*, Steven Covey conveys that in order to be understood, you must first seek to understand. This goes both ways. Some people believe that approximately 70 percent of communication is body language, 20 percent is tone of voice, and 10 percent is the actual words you use. You can see why it is easy to be misunderstood when communicating via e-mail, text message, or voice mail. It is imperative that we slow down and take the time to communicate clearly and effectively. The short-term pain of having the courage to communicate your point clearly far outweighs the massive pain of knowing the misunderstanding still exists.

Think about it. How many times have you regretted taking the time to clearly state your point, then patiently waiting for and working to understand a response? We tend to hold our emotions in, rather than facing them head on and gaining peace of mind.

So I try to choose my words carefully and be honest when faced with a difficult conversation. I don't always succeed, but I try to remember that wise communication is thoughtful communication. Without realizing it, Grandma was teaching me an old Chinese proverb:

"Think twice before saying nothing."

Some Things are Better Left Unsaid

My friend Jeremy has a very bold personality and is known for speaking EVERYTHING that is on his mind. Quite often he offends and even hurts people with his comments. As a result it's hard for him to find and keep friends. Although it is refreshing to have someone willing to speak everything on their mind, sometimes silence is the best form of communication. Grandma reminded me once that, "Silence offends no one."

The trick is finding that gentle balance between direct communication that's helpful and abrupt comments that only hurt. Learning those subtleties can be a lifelong process.

Grandma taught me:

Not everything on your mind needs to be spoken!

Sit Up

All grandmas probably tell their grandchildren to "Sit up straight!" When Grandma would say this, you could see everyone around the table erect their spine like dominoes in reverse. She even influenced the way I teach. In my health courses I've been known to offer an award for students who maintain good posture throughout a whole lecture.

It takes energy to sit up straight. When you are unaware of your posture, you slump. You are holding yourself in what I call "The Lazy Body Position."

In today's sit-down society, naturally maintaining a vital posture position is difficult; it requires strength, flexibility and, most importantly, conscious awareness. If we are in the subconscious state of everyday life, we tend to let gravity rule our bodies. It is easy to slump when standing in line at the post office or sitting in your car or office chair. Maintaining conscious awareness—willing your body to stay erect, in a vital posture position—is all about paying attention. Turning subconscious posture habits into consciously aware ones, is the first step to a good-looking body that is free from pain and projects confidence.

The immediate solution to poor posture is to take Grandma's advice and simply, "Sit up straight!" Better yet, stand up and move!

Good, conscious posture improves circulation, digestion, strength, and many other bodily functions.

Grandma knew what she was talking about, and as a trainer and health instructor I teach the science behind sitting up straight."

VITAL POSTURE POSITION:
Adapted from Suki Munsell Ph.D, President of Dynamic Health and Fitness Institute, Corte Madera, California.

1. SPINE LENGTHENING EXERCISE

Take a deep breath. Cross your hands in front of your belly and imagine you are slowly taking off a t-shirt. As you lift both arms to the sky, slowly exhale, and imagine each vertebra expanding towards the sky. When your arms are all the way up, take in another deep breath, and lower your arms. As you lower your arms, keep your eyes focused forward and imagine your neck getting longer.

2. THE CORE WRAP AND EXPANDING THE RIBS EXERCISE

Place your hand on your belly button, and suck your belly button back a half-inch as you exhale. Slightly engage your stomach muscles, which will help support your spine. Then inhale deeply, putting your fingers on your lower rib cage, and your thumbs on the top of your rib cage just below your chest muscles. As you exhale, visualize the space between your middle fingers and thumbs expanding. Keep your head straight and your hips and shoulders relaxed.

3. BRINGING BACK THE LUMBAR ARCH EXERCISE

With your arms at your sides, place your right hand to the left of your belly button and under your rib. Inhale and lift your left arm to the sky. Visualize the space under your right hand expanding as your left hand goes up. Now lower the left hand and maintain the expanded position. Do the same on the other side. As you do this, you will feel your lower back regaining its natural curve.

4. GAINING CONFIDENCE POSTURE EXERCISE

Bring your arms to your side, thumbs pointing out. Rotate your arms as far back as possible by opening your chest and trying to get your shoulder blades to meet in the middle of your back. Your chest should be out, and your low back arched. Now return your arms to neutral and relax your shoulders back just a bit.

Do it Right Now

Grandma was a woman of action. When she felt she was procrastinating or being a bit lazy, that little voice in her head would say, "Don't wait, do it right now!" She would simply get up and do the project! Whether it was paying the bills, shoveling four inches of fresh snow, or exercising, she would listen to that little voice and do whatever it was right then.

Think of one thing that you really want to do, that you want to finish. Today take one step towards doing that one thing. If it is a new job, make the phone call or drive to the business and get the application. If you need to finish a document for work, start researching the solutions now. If you want to lose ten pounds, push the doughnuts away, put on some walking shoes right now, go for a 30-minute walk, and quit drinking soda. If your yard needs raking, grab the rake and DO IT RIGHT NOW! Even if you only have 20 minutes to do the project, do what you can now!

For more insight on how to break the procrastination habit read Dr. William J. Knaus's book titled "Do It Now."

Grandma taught me:

Discipline and action weigh a little, but regret weighs a ton!

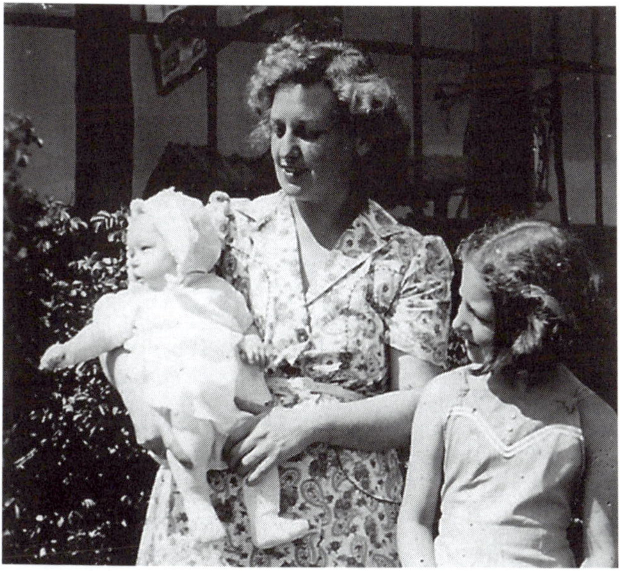

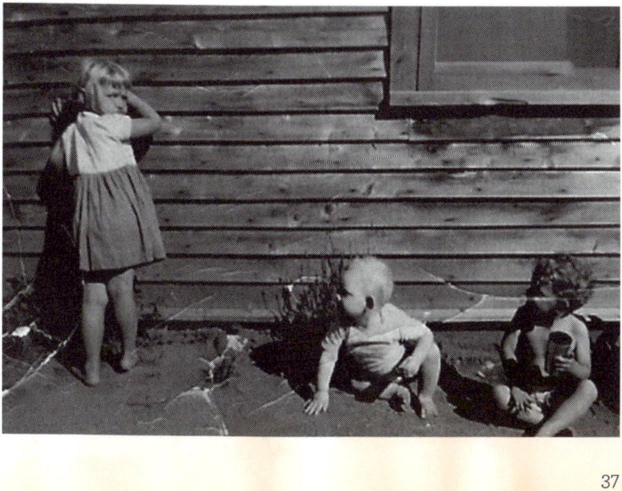

Know Your Body

Several years ago my Grandma went to a highly trained doctor. She complained of constant gas and stomach irritation. The doctor immediately diagnosed her with a terminal problem and told her she had only days to live. Once we heard the news, we gathered at her house, supporting her with our love and concern. Instead of appearing worried and anxious, she sat in her chair completely relaxed.

She truly believed that she had a bad case of gas, not some terminal disease.

We, on the other hand, believed the doctor.

I remember talking to her, telling her how concerned I was. You know what she did? She winked at me and said, "They say I have a day or two to live. The problem is, I don't believe them!"

Come to find out, she was right, and she lived eight more amazing years.

We all have a terminal disease – it's called life. One unknown day you WILL take your last breath. Grandma didn't believe her last day was real until her last day came. Doctors are educated, and they're often smart, wise, valuable resources, but sometimes, like in Grandma's case, they're wrong. Sometimes it's wise to seek second and third opinions about our own bodies. Don't try to be your own physician, but study symptoms and genetic backgrounds, trust your instincts, and advocate for yourself before believing everything a doctor says.

Grandma taught me:

Respect and enjoy your body, and it will provide you all the energy necessary to have fulfilling and fun experiences.

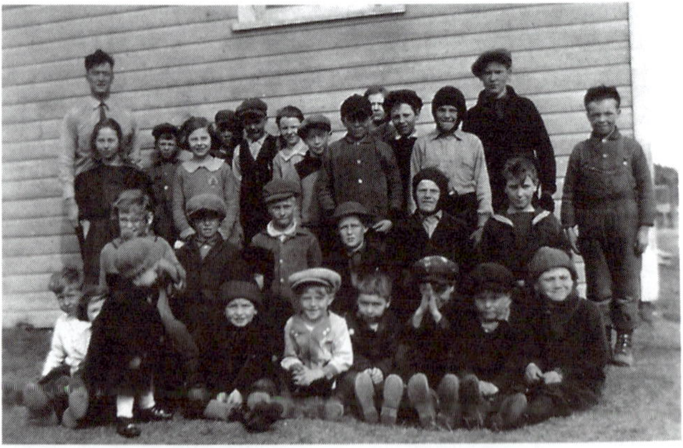

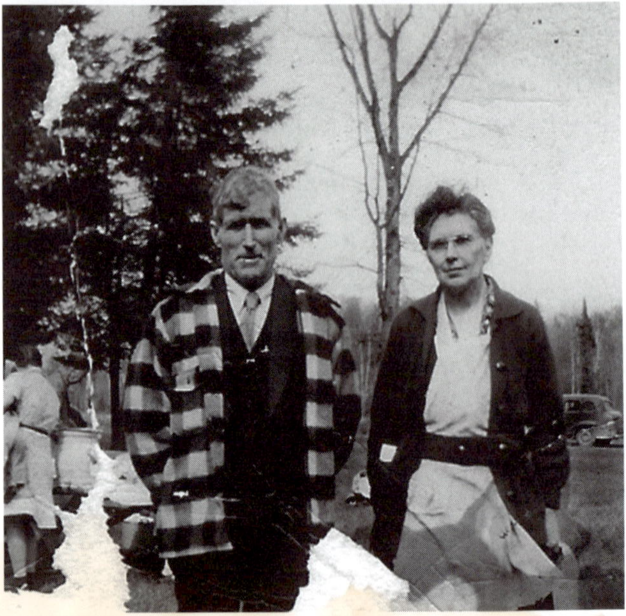

Today is the Day

I remember one time when Grandma was planting flower bulbs in the fall just before the first frost came. She said to me, "I am planting these bulbs now so we all can enjoy beautiful flowers in the spring. The funny thing is, they may never grow! So I am going to enjoy my hands in the dirt today."

Enjoying the moment is the key to life. A wise philosopher once said, "It's not the destination, but the journey itself, that's important." I know most of my students can't wait to graduate. If they learned to enjoy their classes and the process of learning, their college experience would be much richer.

Grandma said:

"I feel sorry for people whose best times were in the past, or who believe that happiness won't happen until the future. For me, today is the best day. Now if you'll excuse me: I have to do my crossword puzzle."

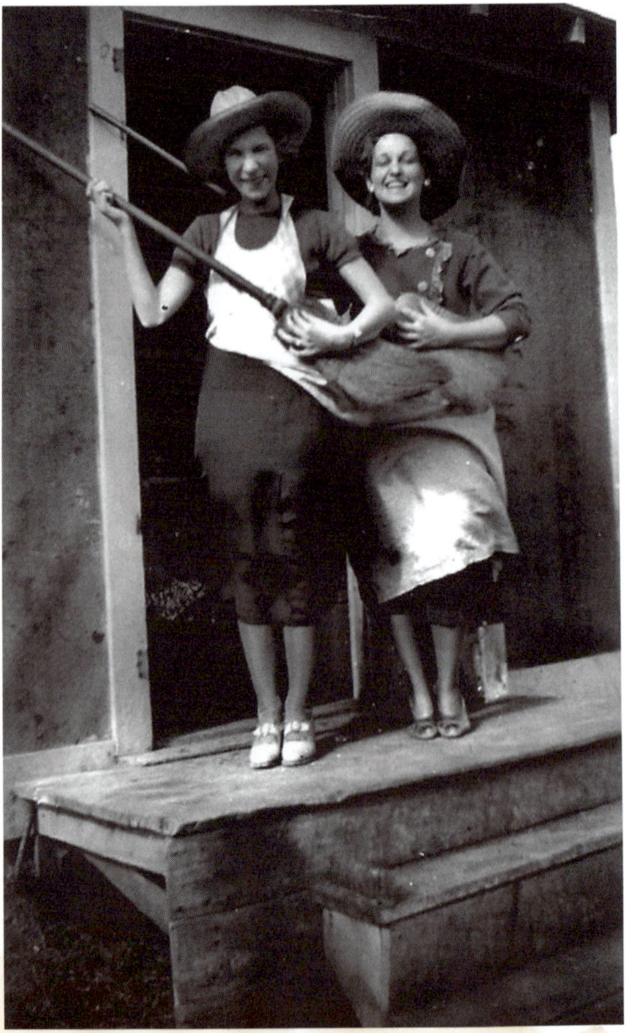

Don't Stay a Beginner

Grandma always loved the challenge of trying new things. She encouraged me to do the same. But sometimes the theory of a challenge is more comfortable than confronting it.

My son Beau is a fantastic piano player. After years of being inspired by him and wanting to learn the instrument, I decided to do it. I was excited. Then I realized how difficult it would be.

I'll never forget my first lesson—I was 33 years old—and ones that followed. I arrived at the music center with a bunch of eight to ten-year-olds who also were waiting for their lesson. Everyone was just as excited as I was.

After two simple lessons I became frustrated with my coordination and inability to learn quickly. When I arrived at my third lesson, an eight-year-old girl was just finishing. She smiled and politely asked me if my lessons were fun.

Fun?

The word hadn't even crossed my mind. More like annoying. Frustrating. I felt like I had two left hands! Being 33 and learning a new musical skill wasn't easy.

Unfortunately, I let my work schedule make it difficult for me to practice before my first piano exam. I tried to jam in a little piano time beforehand, but every musician knows that you just can't cram musical technique. Piano skills have to be built systematically and with discipline. You have to practice at least thirty minutes a day in the beginning just to get to level one!

My last-minute scramble was adult arrogance. As adults, we sometimes assume we can learn anything at any time because of our life experience. And, after all, I was an athlete.

I sat down at my piano exam and gave it the best I'd prepared myself to give.

I failed.

As I walked out of the practice room head down, the cheerful, polite, and friendly eight-year-old was standing there.

"Hi," she said. And then with a confident smile: "I'm on book two. What book are you on?"

Looking down at her, feeling small in my 33-year-old shoes, I did what any adult would do when faced with failure in the presence of youthful success...

I lied.

"I'm going on book three," I said just as confidently as she had. Right then, our teacher walked out, gave me my lesson book, which I had forgotten in the practice room, and said, "Rod, I hope next week you do your lesson, so we can move out of book one." Then she and the little girl, who was giggling, walked into the room.

Grandma taught me:

Enjoying the journey toward a new skill is the secret to mastering it.

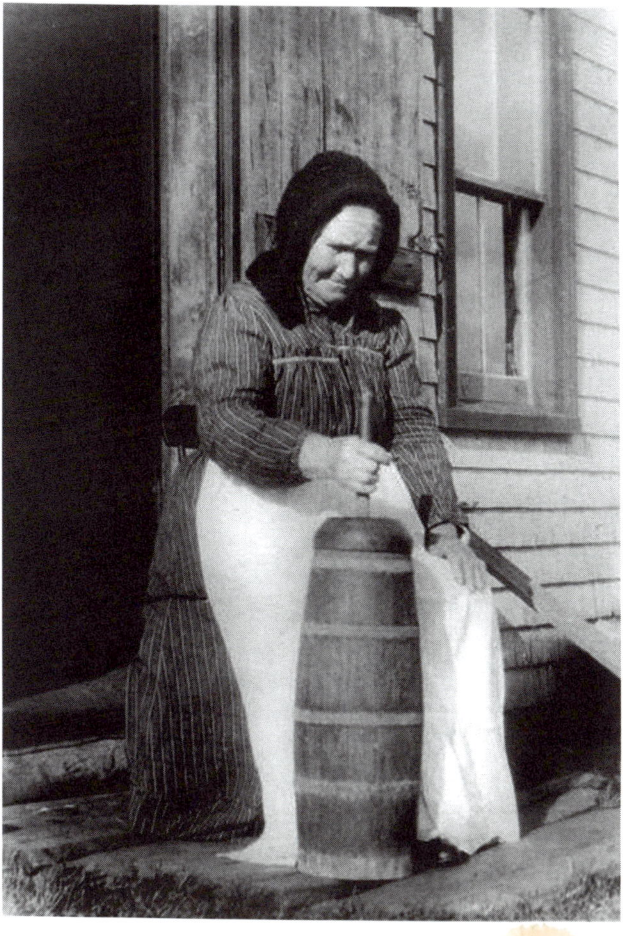

Live a Renaissance Life!

When I was young I played hockey, football, and baseball, learned the guitar, and even took karate lessons. I wasn't great at any one of those activities. Still, as an adult, I can enjoy all those activities with my friends.

Today, kids are often asked to train for and play one sport or activity year round. How does this provide the wide variety of experiences needed to create the renaissance existence Grandma indirectly referred to all her life?

Grandma used to tell us, "Do a lot of different things." Think about it. If you take up guitar lessons for the first time and truly realize what it takes to master the craft, won't watching Eddie Van Halen rock out be more entertaining? If you played hockey and realized what it takes to score three goals, wouldn't watching a professional score five goals just blow you away? The more things you try, the more chances you'll have to learn, grow, and live a vibrant life.

Grandma taught me:

Learning to be pretty good at many different skills is better than mastering just one.

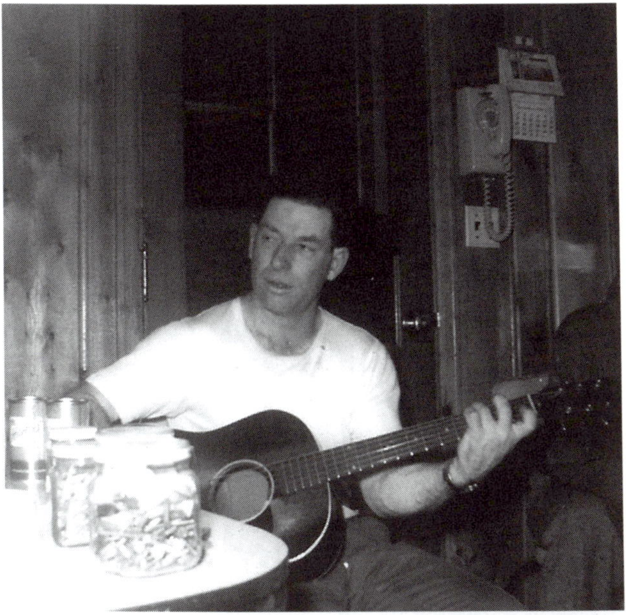

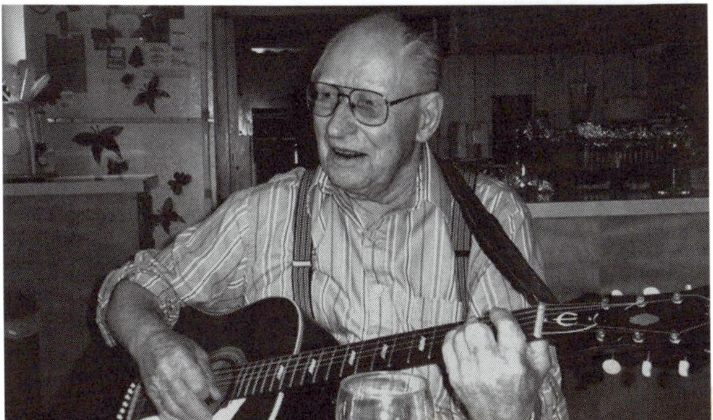

*Silver Creek Cliff - St Road No 1
E.H.W. Two Harbors Minn.
N. Shore Lake Superior.*

Keep Heading North

Grandma often referred to a "compass philosophy," which meant the direction a person is heading depends on how close to their values they're living. She'd say that someone who's generally headed north is on the path to happiness and fulfillment.

Heading "south" on the other hand, meant acting against personal values. Heading south can be tempting sometimes, but living there can lead to unhappiness and even depression.

Grandma would also caution us about being "too north." Too north meant being like an elite athlete: so regimented, and so "by the rules" that we can't possibly live life to the fullest. We have to admit that the occasional piece of cheesecake or a lazy Sunday is food for the spirit!

Balance, moderation, and just having some crazy, out-of-character fun are important.

A few years ago, a friend of mine steered himself due south: cheated on his wife, took to drinking, and made himself miserable. He's never been able to reset his personal compass very far north; he still struggles with personal happiness today.

It takes both discipline and self-forgiveness to avoid living south. Mistakes happen, but after one or two we always have the opportunity to courageously accept our weaknesses, commit to changing what we can, and re-set our compasses.

Hey, we've all strayed a bit south every once in a while! We need to let this southern movement bother us a bit to create just enough stress to make a change. We also need to seek forgiveness from those we may have hurt in the process.

Everyone knows that perfection is impossible. But generally speaking, if we are eating wisely, spending time with those we love, and staying true to our self-identity, we'll be heading north. If we're truly living according to our own values compass, we can wake up tomorrow or six years down the road and say, "Life is guut!"

On a compass, everything above the east-west line is north.

Grandma taught me:

The closer to true north you are, the happier you'll be. But don't go too far that direction, if you know what I mean!

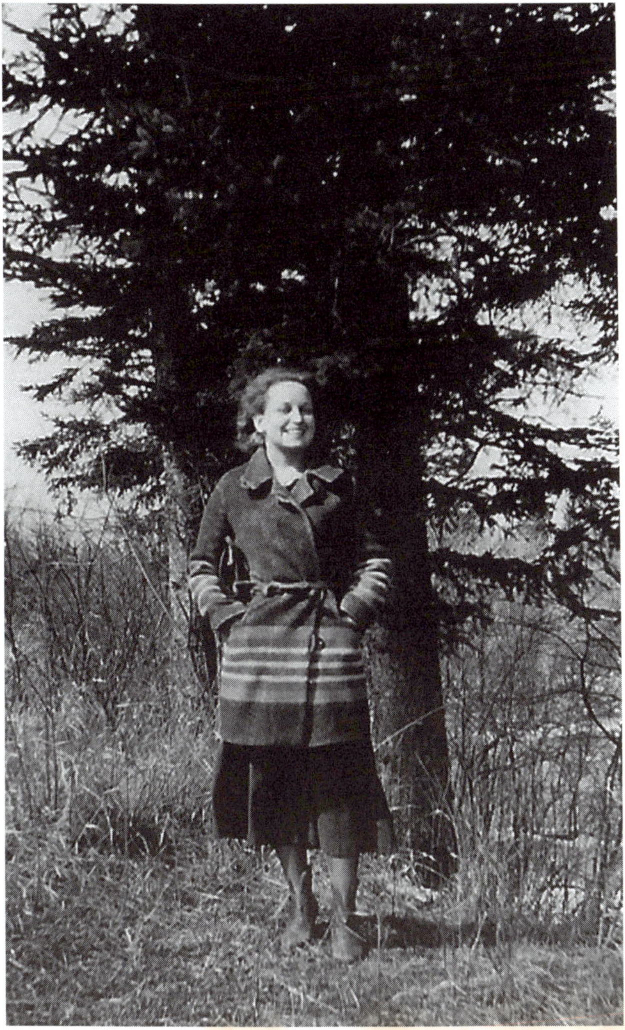

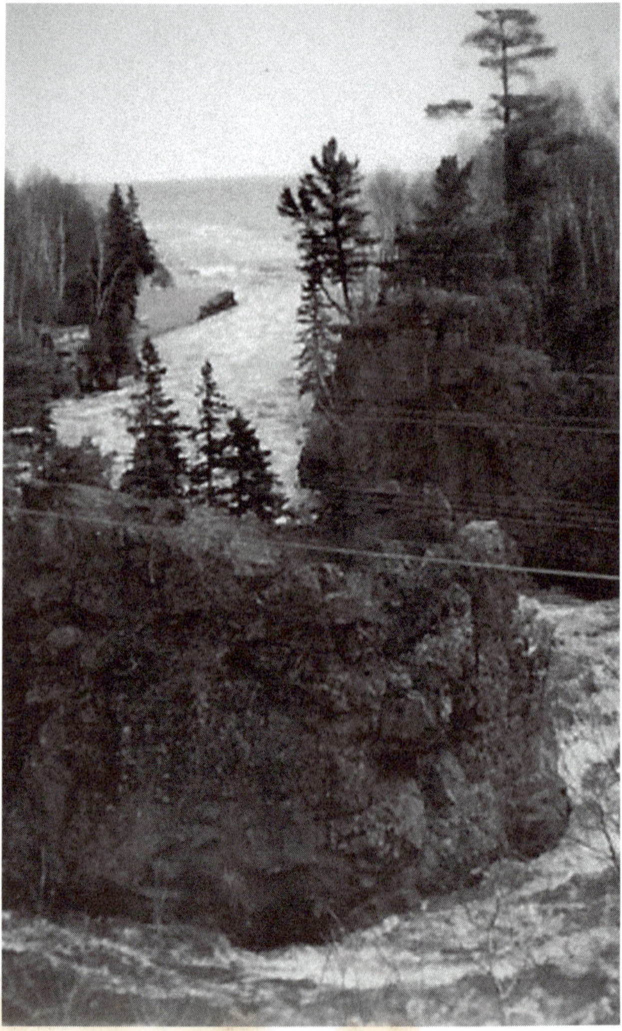

53

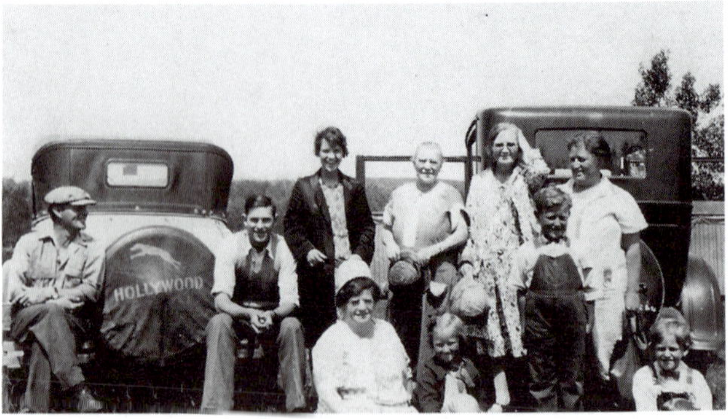
HOLLYWOOD

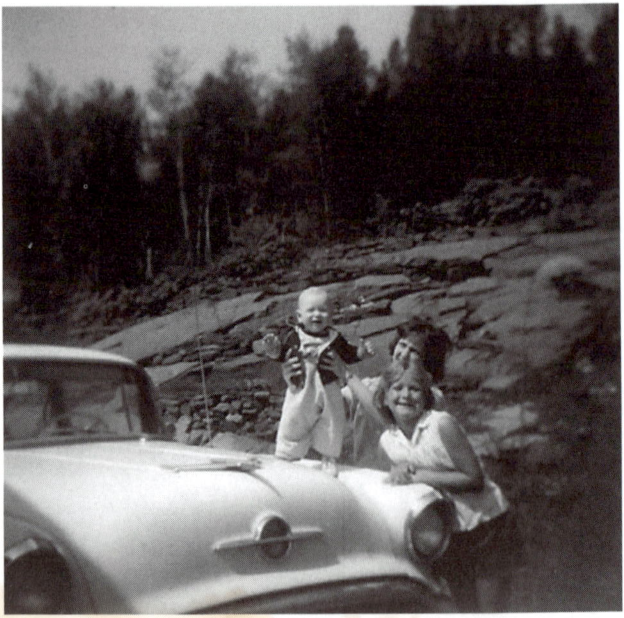

Travel When You're Young

Don't wait till you're in your seventies to see the world.

By 1965, Grandma and Grandpa closed the Trading Post, and Grandpa went to work for Reserve Mining, the iron ore operation in Silver Bay, Minnesota. With her newfound time, Grandma became the village clerk and could also enjoy her favorite pastime: reading books on all sorts of topics.

She read from the complete works of Winston Churchill to romance novels. When asked if she would like to be a world traveler she replied, "I've seen the world through books."

Grandma didn't leave Beaver Bay, Minnesota, for any extended travel until my Grandpa retired. Then they did what many retired folks do: they bought a motor home and went to Florida. After a few months of the Sunshine State, they wanted to come back home.

After all, their friends, family, and grandchildren were back in northern Minnesota. Grandma said Florida was too busy, and she had too much trouble walking to truly dive into culture and sights.

That lesson and others taught me to be curious and motivated to explore far-away lands and try new things.

I was 19 when I first took to the friendly skies on my way to Hawaii.

Many people around the world visit Hawaii to take in its sights and learn a thing or two about surfing; I happened to be there for the Ironman Triathlon. When I was accepted into the world's toughest race (a 2.4 mile swim, 112 mile bike and 26.2 mile run), I knew I would never forget the journey. While the race was important, simply being there inspired me. I was doing the race because Grandma told me to travel when I was young.

Her worldly inspiration has since taken me to Thailand's Buddhas, Australia's Outback, New Zealand's lush vegetation, Canary Islands' volcanic landscape, Scotland's highlands, Costa Rica's surfing beaches, Western Canada's mountains, and Brazil's tropical rain forests. I have amazing friends in Switzerland, Germany, Chili, and France. I was anointed a New Foundland Screecher (you have to go to find out what this is), and I hiked the Italian Alps. I have these experiences and others because Grandma strongly told me that it's important not only to see the world, but to dive into its many cultures and people.

Grandma taught me:

It's a big world. See it from your feet, not from a mobile home or TV screen!

Finding reasons not to travel is easy. But time continues to tick, and opportunities are everywhere. Browse Internet travel sites, walk past a travel agency and pick up a brochure. Order tourist information from places you're curious about. Put your bike in your car and start moving. Go somewhere new. When you get there, bike around the area. It's the best way to see the landscape. When you change your scenery, you change your perspective on a lot of things. Just don't stay home; motion creates emotion-- see the world!

Grandma taught me:

If you want your life to change, you must change. Start by changing what you see – travel!

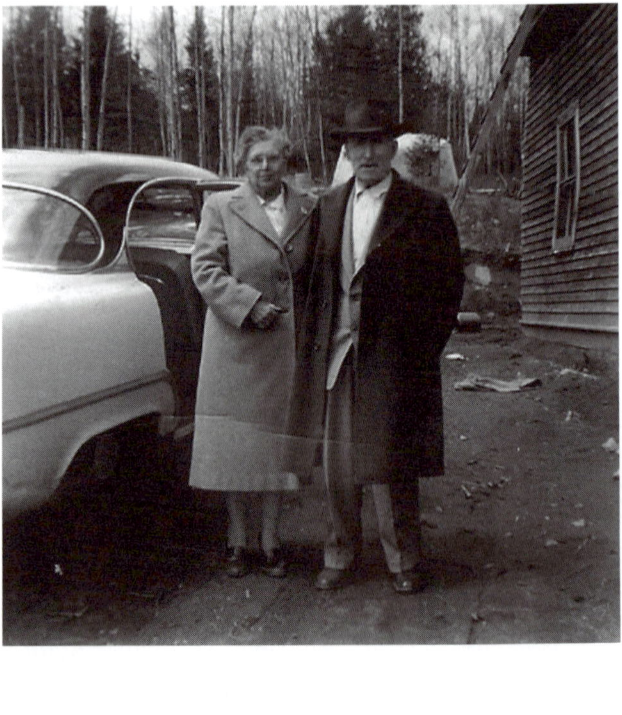

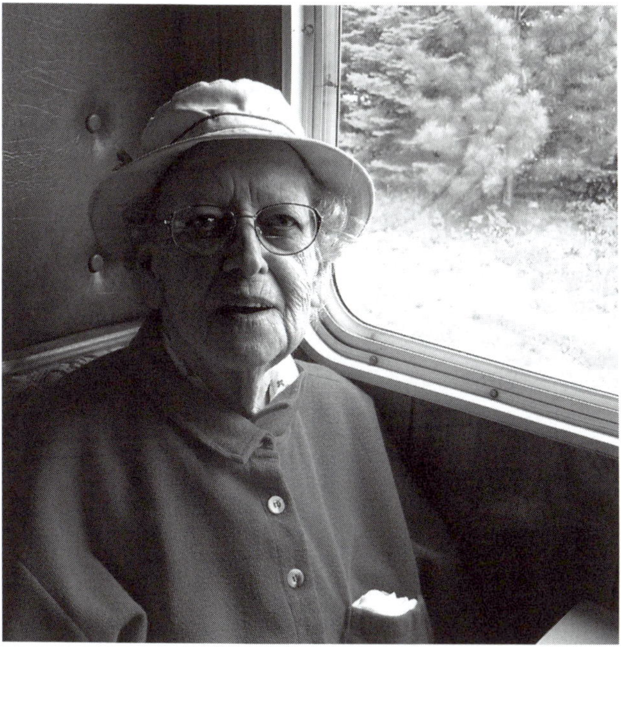

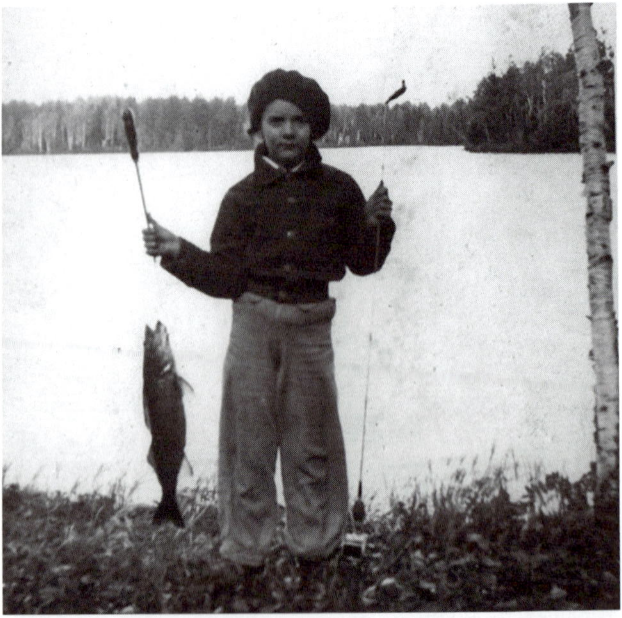

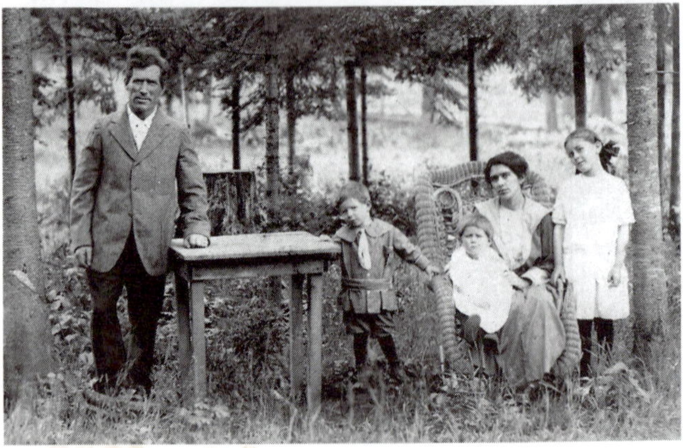

Go Fishin' Often

Grandma believed that few things in life are more simple, more spiritual, more healing, and more fun than a good day fishin'.

One summer, Grandma, Grandpa, and the rest of my family met and camped together near the Boundary Waters Canoe Area Wilderness (BWCAW) in northern Minnesota. As we were sitting around the fire, we noticed other kids buzzin' around on their ATVs. I could see the stress in Grandma's eyes as the noisy machines kept circling around and around. She said to me, "You need to do your best to keep areas like this pristine and quiet." She was talking softly so she didn't offend anyone. She knew that I wouldn't judge her on this.

My son wanted to go on the four-wheelers as well. I took him for walk in the pine forest instead, and we did parabolic ears (cupping your hands behind your ears, carefully listening to every sound the forest makes). He thought that was so cool. He described different natural sounds of the forest.

The Wilderness Act of 1964 was created to " ... Secure for the American People of present and future generations the benefit of an enduring resource of Wilderness...." The BWCAW is one among many places in our country that is protected by this Act. It is our privilege to visit these places, our gift to enjoy them.

In today's non-stop, constantly on-the-go world, it's hard to find peace of mind. It's unfortunate that we have to work so hard to find silence and reconnect with nature. But no matter where you live, you can find or create a place that offers solitude from civilization, even if it's just lying on your back in the grass so you can see nothing but the sky.

Do you realize that if you're 50 years old and you take one trip a year with your kids, your friends, or your spouse, you might only have about 20 trips left?

Give your mind and body the reward of natural meditation. Grandma called it her vitamin W - vitamin wilderness.

The key to finding this peace and solitude is to change your perspective. Going fishing or stepping into a forest for a day might seem frivolous, easily exchanged for a higher priority commitment. That just isn't true. Grandma and Grandpa would go to the wilderness as a part of living, not as an escape from living.

Grandma taught me:

Make connection to nature part of your daily life—and bring kids with ya!

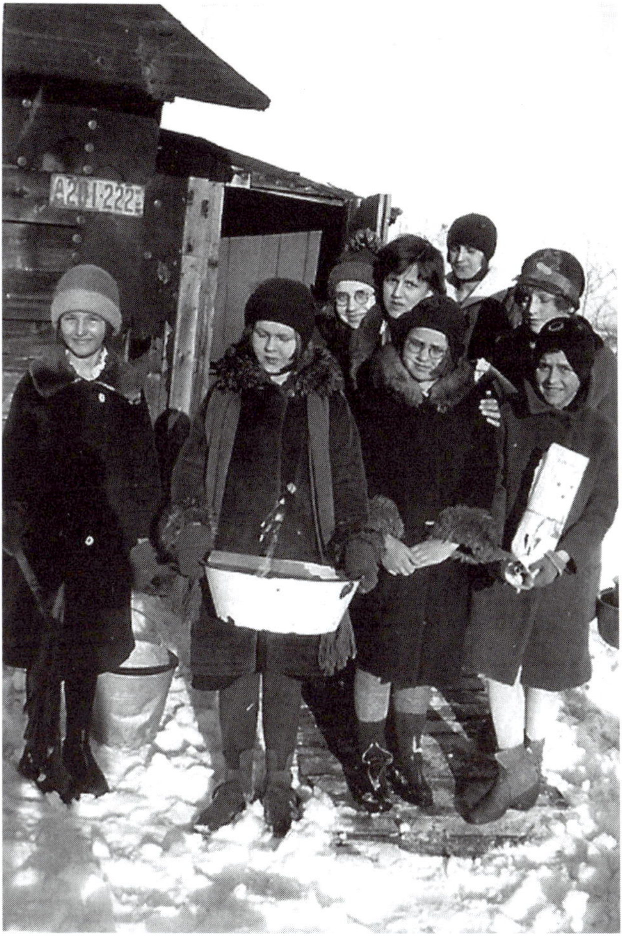

Love Animals like Brothers and Sisters

Grandma had a simple philosophy about wild animals: "We need to save as much natural space as we can for all the critters to eat and sleep." She also believed in management of species and wasn't too hung up on either extreme. She simply treated animals with great respect, and valued them as much as she valued her human neighbors.

Grandma taught me:

Protect the wild; our children and grandchildren need it.

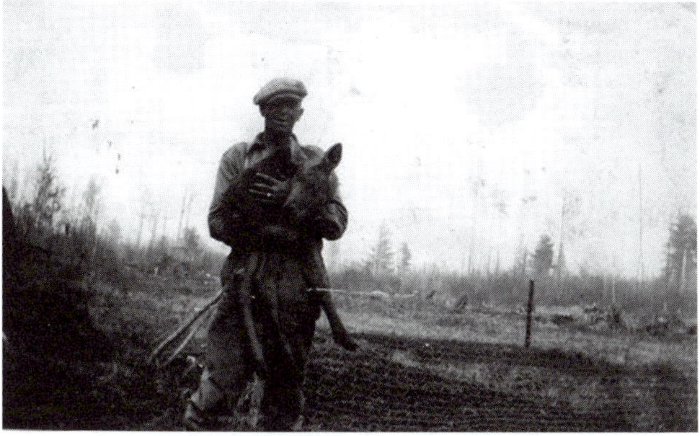

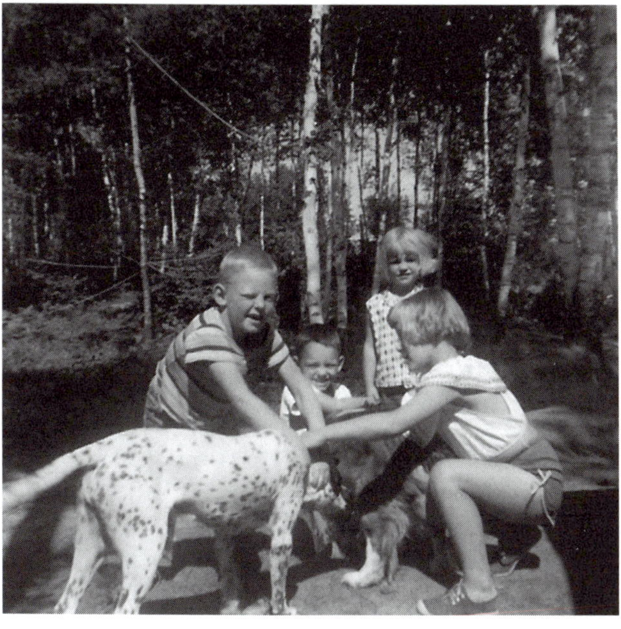

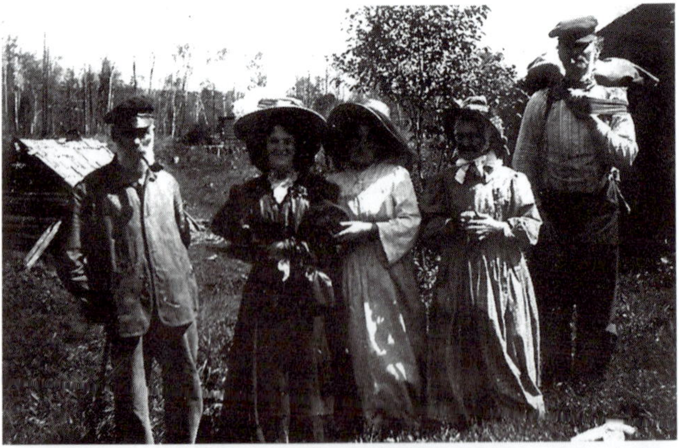

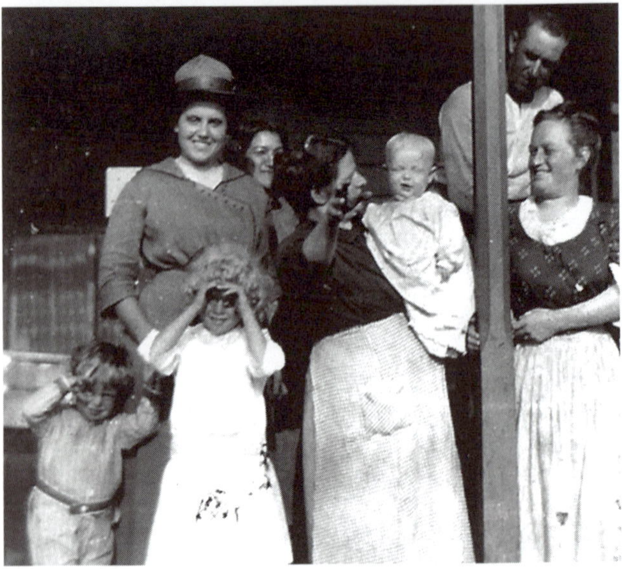

Never go to a Social Event on an Empty Stomach

It's a simple idea, but with great insight.

Being a university instructor, I often find myself at banquets and social functions. When I arrive I look around for the food table. I usually see some crackers and cheese, some veggies and fruit, and maybe some cookies. If I don't eat before going to these functions, I find myself filling my little paper plate to the rim and going back many times. It's hard to socialize when I'm trying to eat a full meal! Not only that, but the food at these events tends to be unhealthy.

I've thought about this and remembered Grandma's teachings. Social events are meant to be social, not nutritional. Now I try to eat a little something before going to parties. That way, I don't have my head on a swivel looking to see if all those little wieners are gone.

Grandma taught me:

Your stomach doesn't like to be empty. Keep it topped off, but never get so full that it hurts.

Meet Someone New Every Day

There's a saying: "In order to have friends, you must first show that you're friendly."

It takes little effort to meet someone new every day. Reach your hand out first when you run into a stranger. Strike up a conversation while waiting in line. Invite a new co-worker out for a bite to eat. Let go of any social fears or pride you may have. People need people. Think about it: by being just a bit more outgoing, you could make 365 new friends every year.

Grandma taught me:

Humility is Godlike; timidity is unfortunate.

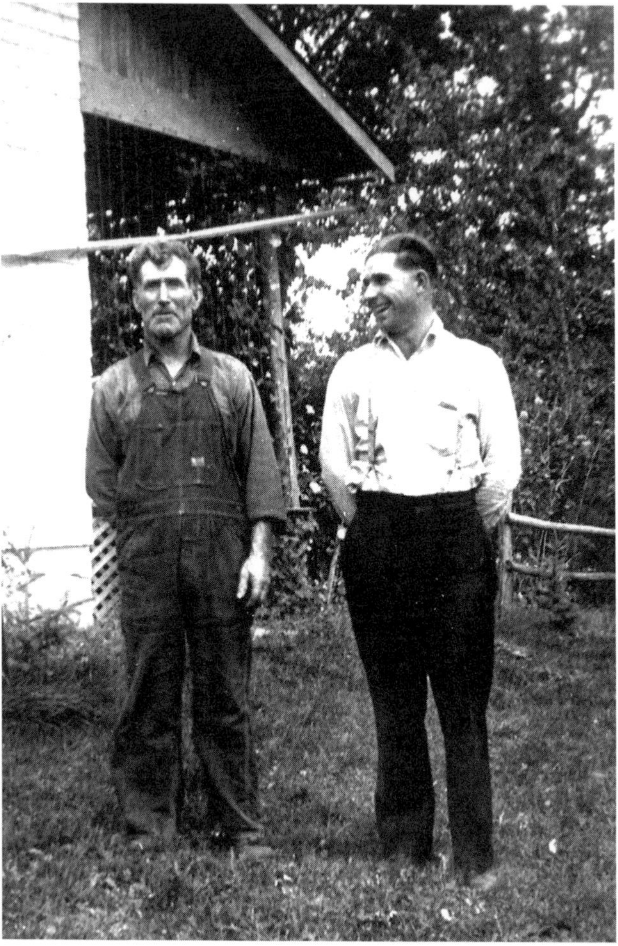

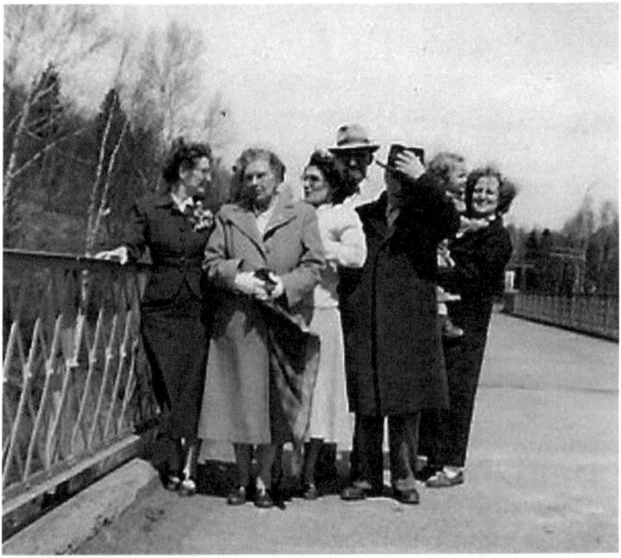

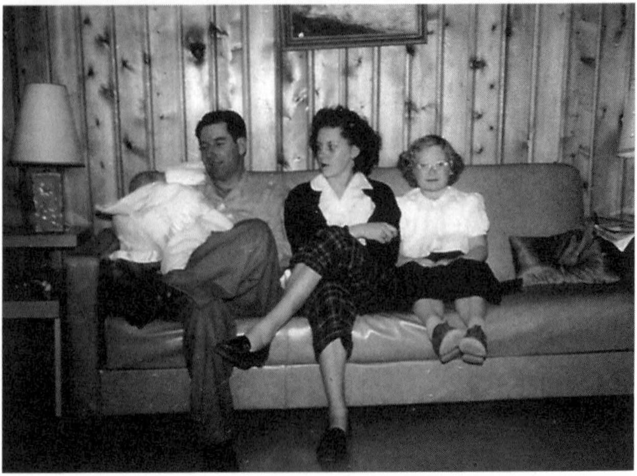

Put People Before Money

Grandma gave me the best financial advice I've ever received: she taught me to always place people before money and to live within my means.

Anyone who pays attention to human nature and history knows that no 80-year-olds wish they'd have spent more time making money and less time investing in human relationships. The adage "You came into this world naked and you leave this world naked" always proves itself true. But let's be real: sometimes there is more month than money; and taking care of yourself and your family requires you to work. The secret is finding the balance between financial security and rich life experiences.

Grandma grew up during the hard times, when money was scarce and credit was nonexistent. She spent a part of her childhood at her grandparents' hotel on the banks of the Beaver River, overlooking Lake Superior. When the hotel burned down, they moved to what was then called the Indian House. It was a building the Native Americans used for a summer dwelling, so it had no insulation.

In order to build a restaurant that included living quarters for his family, Grandma's father first retrieved logs that went astray while being transported on Lake Superior, then worked the logs till they were his business and home. In those days, as Grandma said, it was, "Make do, or do without."

Today, if my water heater breaks and I'm short on cash, I can take out my credit card and charge a new one. Interesting how things have changed since Grandma's time. In Grandma's day, I'd just have to go without hot water until I earned the money to buy a new one (of course, hot water on demand wasn't an option in her day). Wisdom from her times helps me balance my life today. Like many of our inventions, credit is a useful thing in emergencies, but going in debt is not a wise way of life.

Money doesn't care who has it. It just "hangs out." Make sure you have a plan on how you manage yours. If you don't have some sort of a financial plan, then you may find yourself planning on how to live broke.

I had a friend who once bought a large boat. He was so busy working to pay for it that he was only able to use it 3 or 4 times a summer. The cost to own, maintain, and rent space for this boat was enormous. It may have made him look wealthy, but it was draining his pocket book and the experience was not fulfilling.

He didn't want the boat as much as he wanted the *feelings* he hoped that boat would bring him.

Grandma taught me:

People don't judge you by your stuff—they judge you by the substance of your stories and experiences.

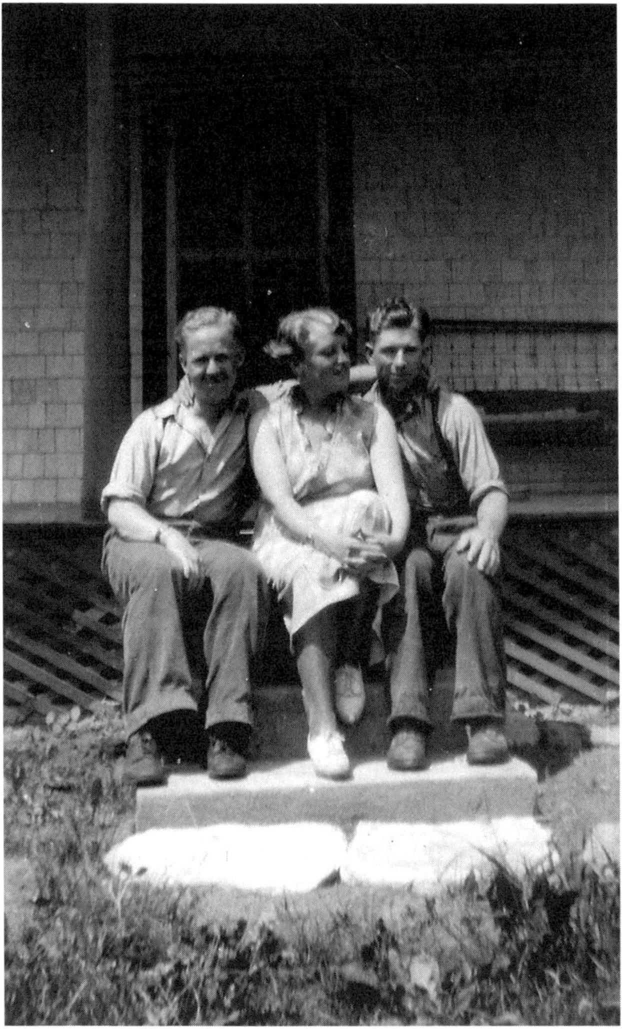

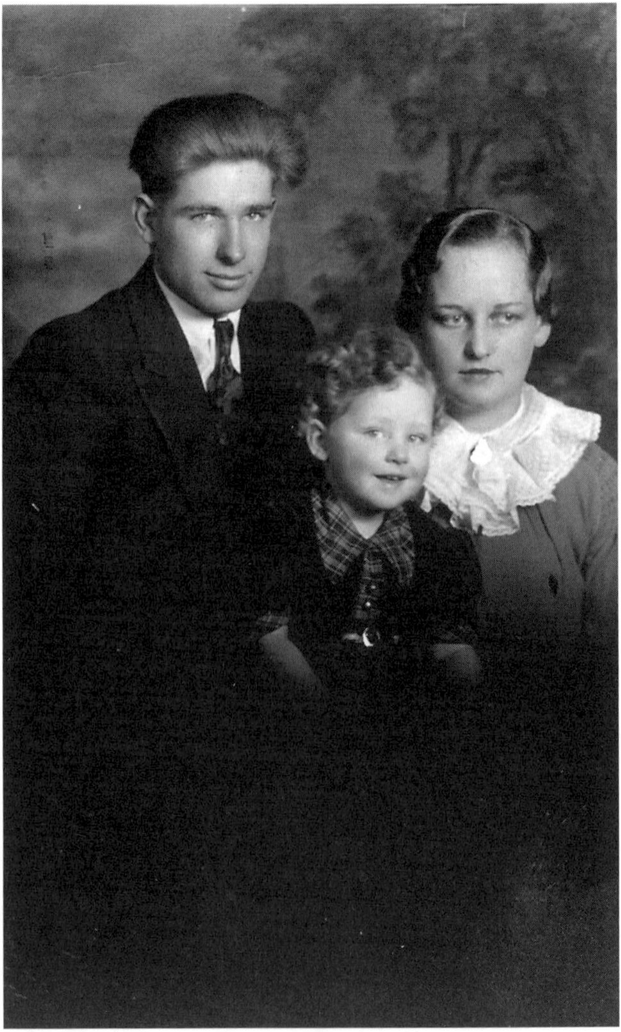

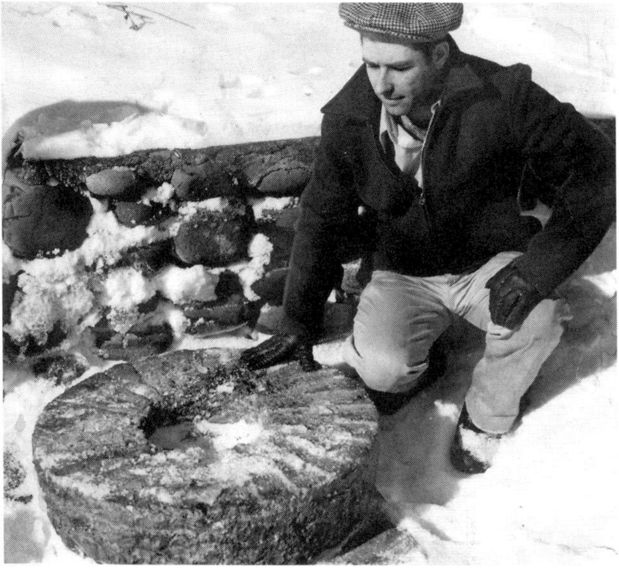

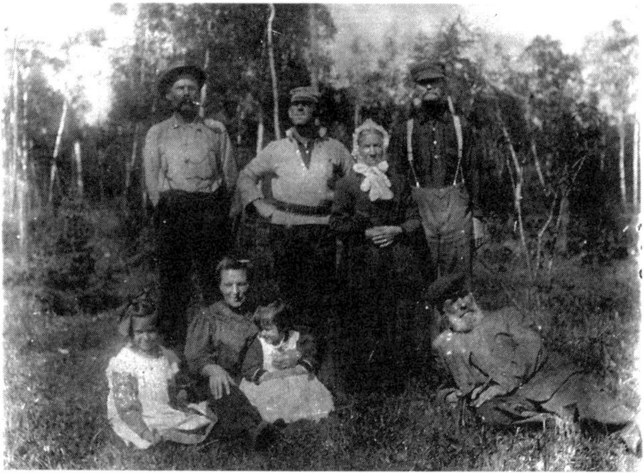

Don't Stir the Poop

Stirring the poop won't make it smell any better.

Grandma used to tell the story of how Grandpa, after butchering a deer, threw the parts he didn't use into Lake Superior. The remains landed in her great grandfather's fishing nets. When Great Grandpa Oscar went to pull up his catch, the hide and hooves and antlers were all tangled up in the nets and were destroying them.

When Grandpa showed up, Great Grandpa Oscar said, "If I ever get a hold of the guy who threw this carcass in here, I will beat the tar out of him!"

Grandpa, in his wisdom said, "I would beat him, too!"

When Grandma told us that story we all laughed. When we were done laughing, she shared with us the principle she learned from her Grandpa.

Grandma taught me:

Say it if it will heal. Don't say it if it will cause pain.

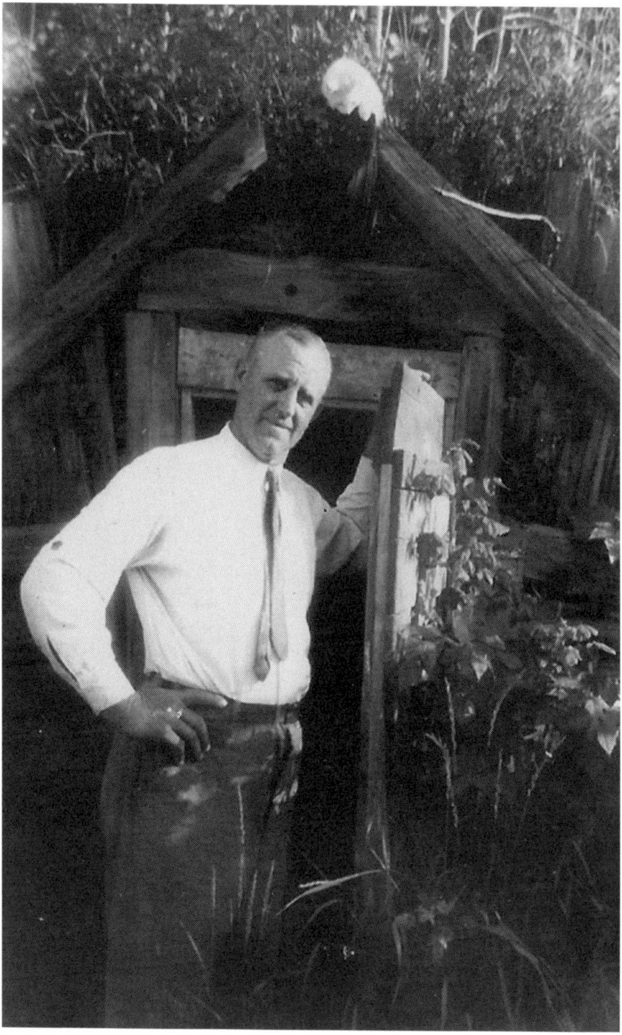

Don't Be an Outhouse, Flush it Away

Sometimes I find myself in a negative situation with other people. Emotions fly high and maybe feelings get hurt. In these situations, I try to remember to back away and take a breath. Go for a walk. Chill out. Try to see the situation from the other person's point of view.

I used to get angry with my "ex" for myriad reasons. Grandma taught me, "Rod, it's just stuff, and when you are in your 80s, like I am, you won't care! Let it go."

She was right, of course. And after I learned to let go, I felt a huge release in my stomach, as though I stopped an accelerated aging process. It was truly a great moment!

My Grandma taught me that if I keep nagging on another person, the situation will only get worse. She told me to quit obsessing; some things are better left unsaid. After all, as Grandma said, sooner or later we are all going to leave this planet, and all the petty things won't matter anymore.

Grandma taught me:

People remember you by how you made them feel. Help make them feel good!

Bury the Hatchet

"And don't leave the handle sticking out of the ground!"

Maxwell Garrison moved from Northhome, Minnesota, to Lake Superior's North Shore to work in a Civilian Conservation Corps camp in the early 1930s. Not long after, Grandma's brother, who also worked in the camp, brought home his friend Max. Grandma captured Max's heart–they were married on February 9, 1935, and spent the next 72 years enjoying what life had to offer. They were a great team. They hunted, fished, trapped, snow-shoed, made maple syrup, harvested wild rice, and could live off the land if necessary. Grandpa made his fair share of mistakes when he was younger, all of which Grandma forgave. She would tell you herself: no relationship is perfect.

It isn't possible to always get along. That's just human nature. We have random disagreements with friends, co-workers, sometimes complete strangers. If we don't argue occasionally, then we're not being honest. Most of the time we find a way to settle the disagreement. We find a way to compromise. And sometimes we have to walk away because we just can't see how to work it out.

Do you react to a disagreement the same way with your spouse as you do with your friends?

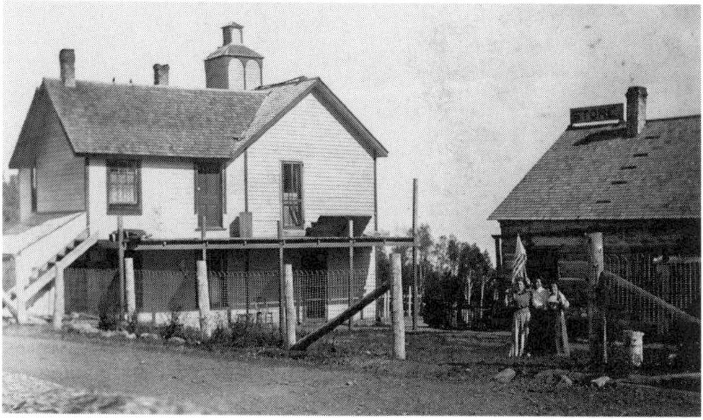

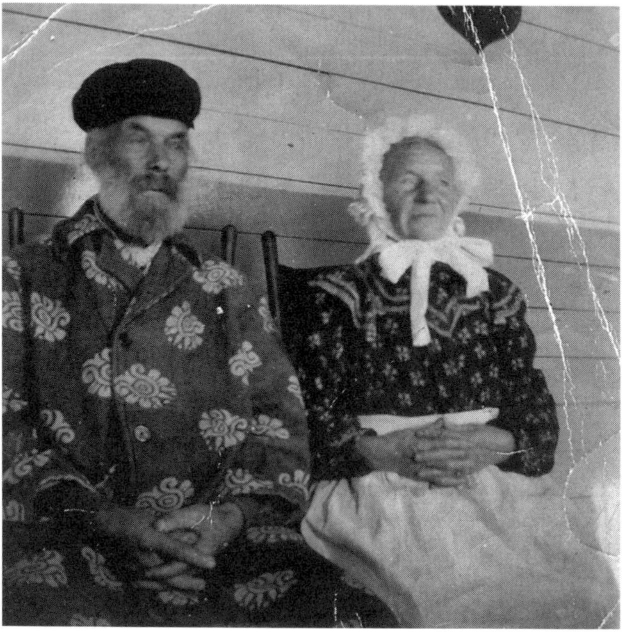

Both Grandma and Grandpa made mistakes during their early years that caused sadness, anger, and disappointment that in today's world would have led to a divorce. But Grandma and Grandpa were two pieces of the same soul.

Because they had the love, genuine friendship, and hope, they were able to sincerely apologize to and forgive each other.

Grandma taught me:

Be competitive about saying "I'm sorry" first.

Apologizing first not only cleans your plate, but it can also help the person you are saying sorry to feel special. By humbling your own spirit and creating positive feelings during a negative moment, you are, in essence, healing a wound.

Today, some research suggests, more than half of all marriages end in divorce. That's not good. What if we believed, like Grandma and Grandpa did, that unless the situation is severe, we need to try to find it in our hearts to forgive our significant others.

Grandma taught me:

Forgive! And pretend to forget.

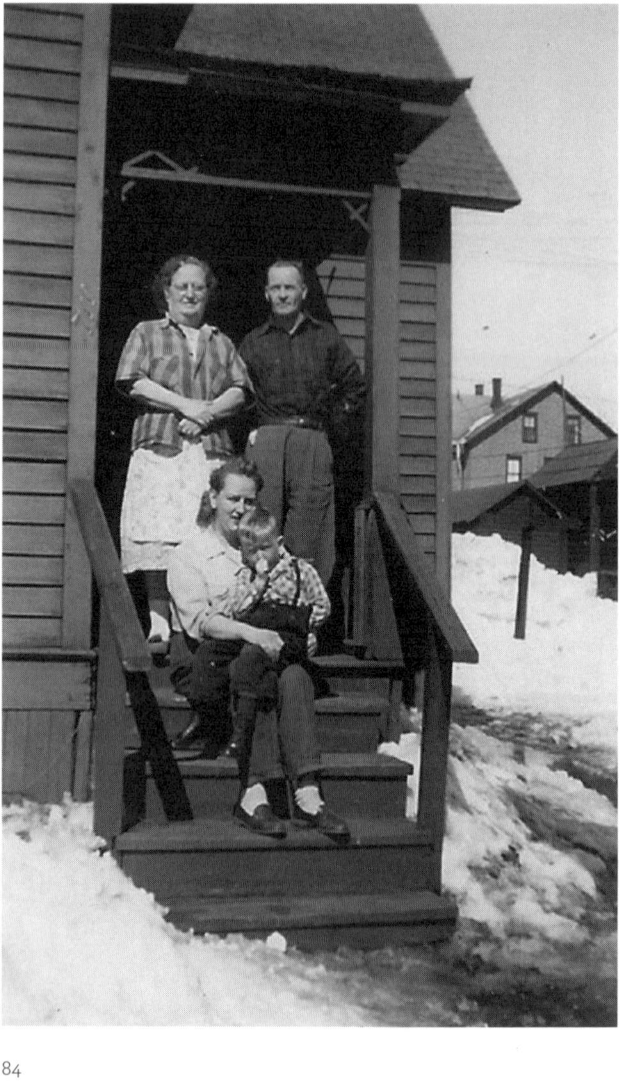

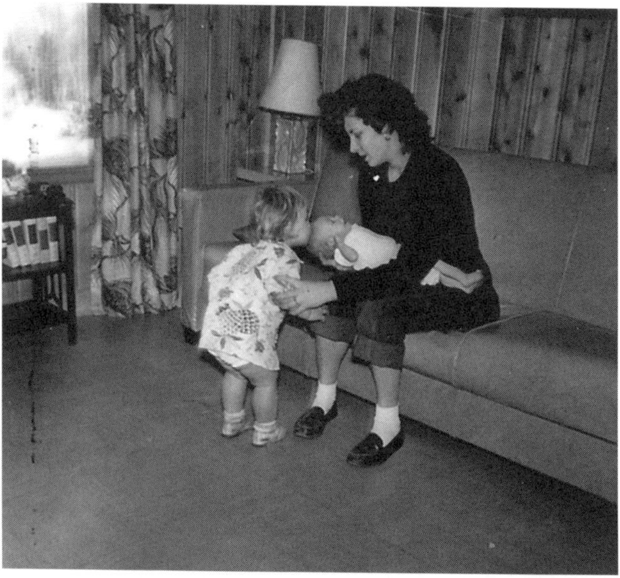

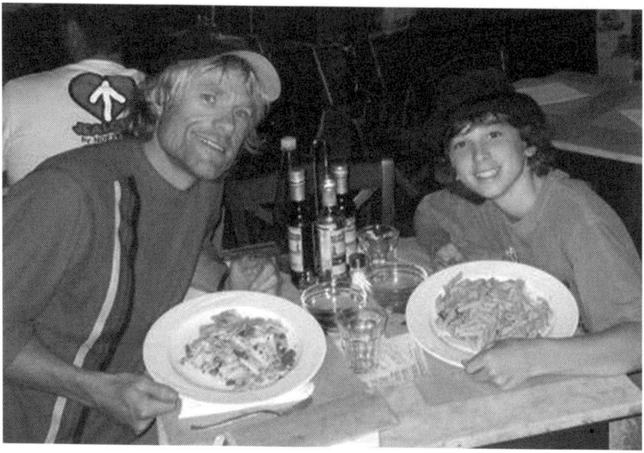

If You Can't Eat it, Toss It!

Don't let negative thoughts and ideas take up real estate in your brain.

It's very common to let a negative co-worker, family members or friend take up your thoughts. We've all experienced something that we can't let go or that eats away at our mood all day. But someone or something like that, especially if we can't do anything about it, needs to be released and forgotten.

Grandma was a genius at letting things go. "If you can't eat it, toss it!" she used to say about problems.

Grandma was not afraid to toss anything.

The Trading Post had a bar that was a popular spot for locals. She once told a story about a drunk who came stumbling in: "He was so drunk that I pulled his hat over his eyes, grabbed the back of his trousers, lifted as hard as I could, and tossed him straight out the BACK DOOR! As I wiped my hands clean, Susie, the other waitress, said, 'How much do you want to bet he comes back in the front door?' A few minutes passed, and sure enough the man stumbled into the front door. As he leaned on the posts, Susie and I opened the door and the man said, 'Do you two S.O.B.'s work in every bar in this town?'"

Negativity was something Grandma had no time or room for.

I've learned that a good way to let go of negative thoughts is to write them down on paper, or go for a long run or bike. Once I have them on paper I can see them and then consciously let them go. I can toss the paper, I can burn it, and I can draw a smiley face or Mickey Mouse ears on it.

If the thought persists, then I need to persist, and repeat the process of writing it down or moving my body and letting it go.

Grandma taught me:

If you can do something about it, then do it. If not, toss it!

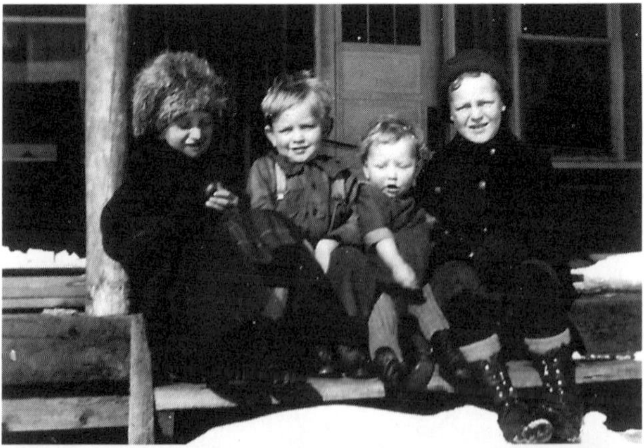

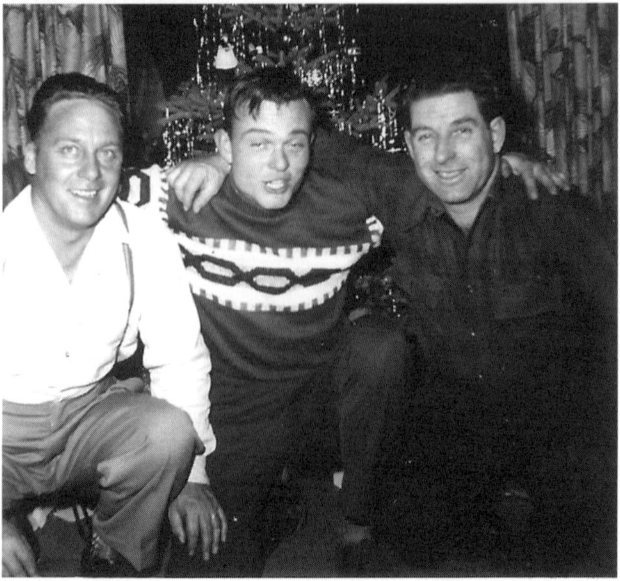

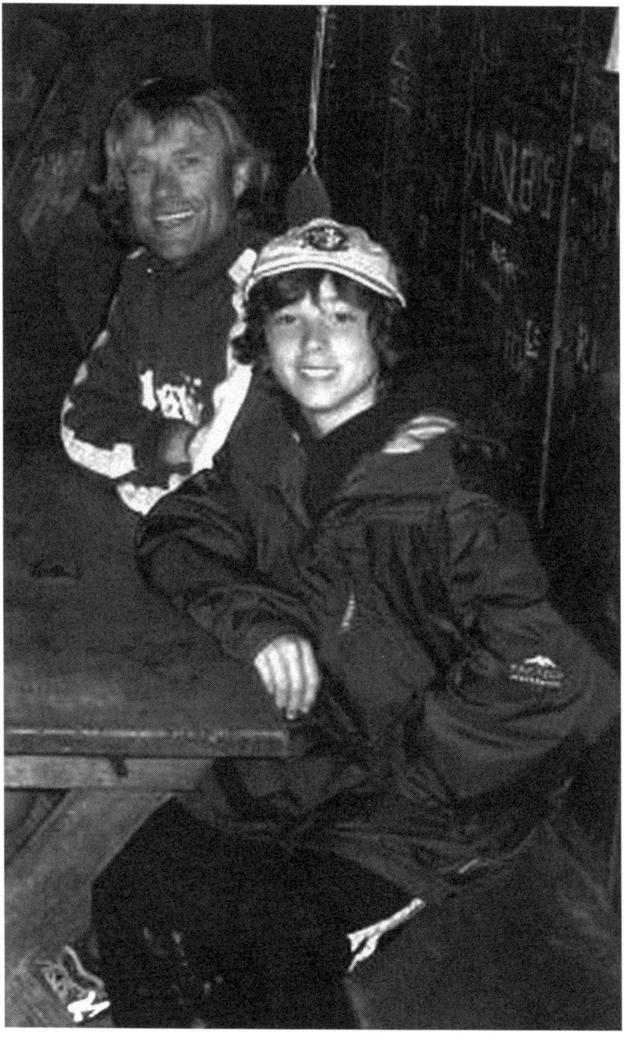

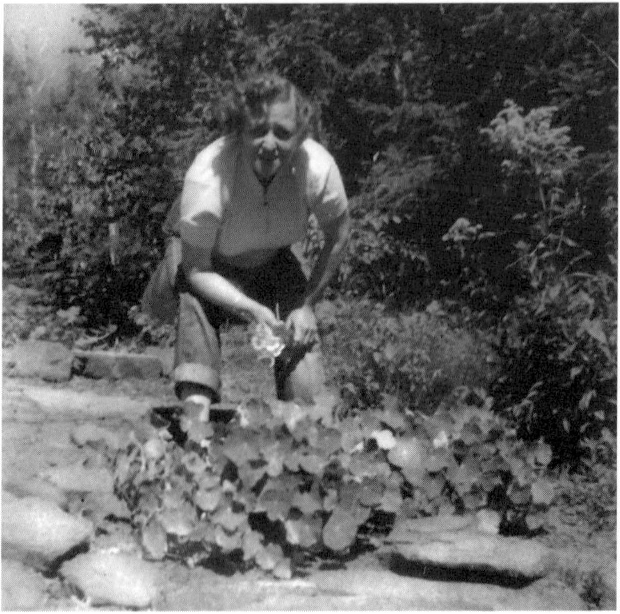

Eat Your Vegetables

Growing vegetables on the rocky North Shore of Lake Superior takes time and commitment. The growing season is short, and the first frost can catch you by surprise.

By advising us to eat our vegetables, Grandma may have been seeking appreciation for her gardening efforts. Nonetheless, like almost everyone's grandma, she knew that kids who eat their vegetables are healthier and stronger.

Modern medicine long ago verified Grandma's beliefs with scientific proof. Generations of us kids now know, beyond a doubt, that Grandma wasn't trying to be mean by forcing those peas on us.

She was just trying to love us and to provide some nutrition for our little growing bodies.

Generally speaking, when we eat vegetables and fruits, we give our bodies the vitamins and minerals they need for daily function. The fiber from skins of organic, chemical-free fruits and veggies is necessary for healthy digestion, among other bodily processes. At the same time, they're helping us fight off quite a few cancers, other diseases, and less-serious ailments.

Don't believe that taking a vitamin is an alternative for real food. Today's research is finding that many natural chemicals found in veggies and fruits cannot be replicated in a single vitamin.

Another important thing to remember: Variety is key.

While grocery shopping, many of us buy the same stuff. We buy some apples and oranges, some carrots and lettuce, some cheese and milk and eggs and some hamburger and chips. Same old, same old! That type of shopping could be worse—at least it's better than believing that potato chips alone will fulfill all your veggie needs!

But scientific research says having a wide variety of fruits and vegetables, hormone-free meats, non-processed grains, chemical free dairy, and pure water over an extended period of time is the key to optimal health. Bottom line, eat foods that are as "close to the earth" as possible!

Grandma taught me:

Eat what Grandma and Grandpa ate: real food!

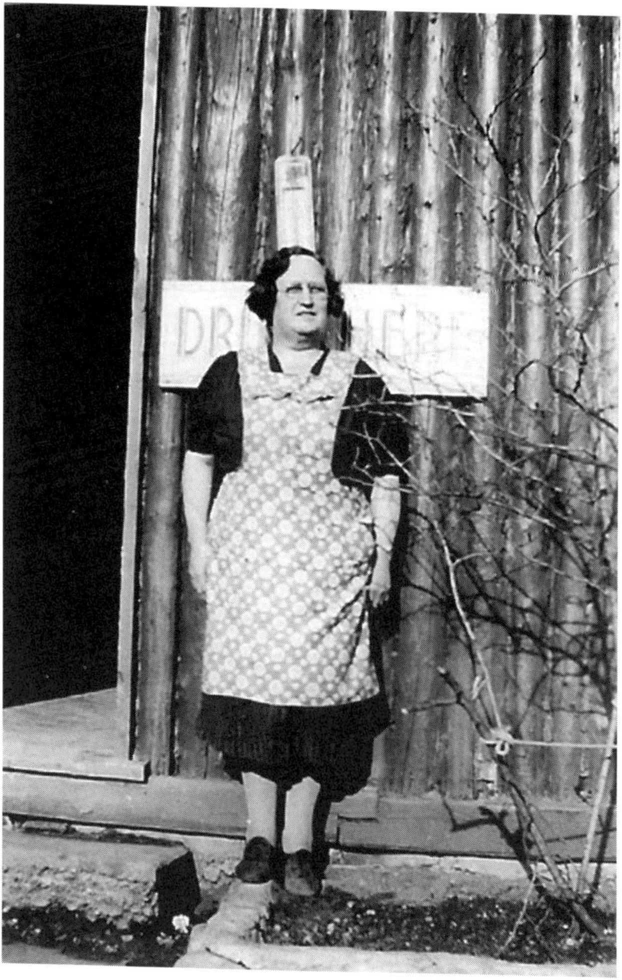

Grow a Garden

Grandma never went to church. But if there ever was a sanctuary worth visiting two times a week for spiritual food, it was her garden!

Grandma and Grandpa's garden wasn't a hobby, or just "for fun." It grew the best food around, and their effort, skill, and planning lead to some of the best home-cooked meals I have ever had.

There is pride in growing. A sense of self-sufficiency that says, "Hey, I worked this soil, I planted that seed, I watered those leaves, and now I can enjoy the fruits of my labor."

Every year at the end of the growing season, Grandma and Grandpa and various family members would go through the ritual of canning and storing the food. It would take days to can the tomatoes, pickle the cucumbers, and store the potatoes. I will never forget those pickles!

It doesn't take much to start a personal garden.

The important thing to ask yourself is, how much space do you have, and how much time do you want to spend? Growing a few items to make salsa and salad would be very cool.

And if you're busy like me, then I have just the plan for you.

Find a patch of land (or four or five big pots), and clear it of grass and weeds. Buy some good mulching material and generously spread it over your patch. Take your shovel and mix the earth with the mulch. Water until drenched. Put in a couple of tomato plants, basil, cilantro, lettuce, and a few carrots. Water your garden daily.

There are few things greater in life than sitting down to a meal that you grew with your own two hands!

Grandma taught me:

Ignore your garden and the weeds will take over.

(I think she was teaching me two lessons here.)

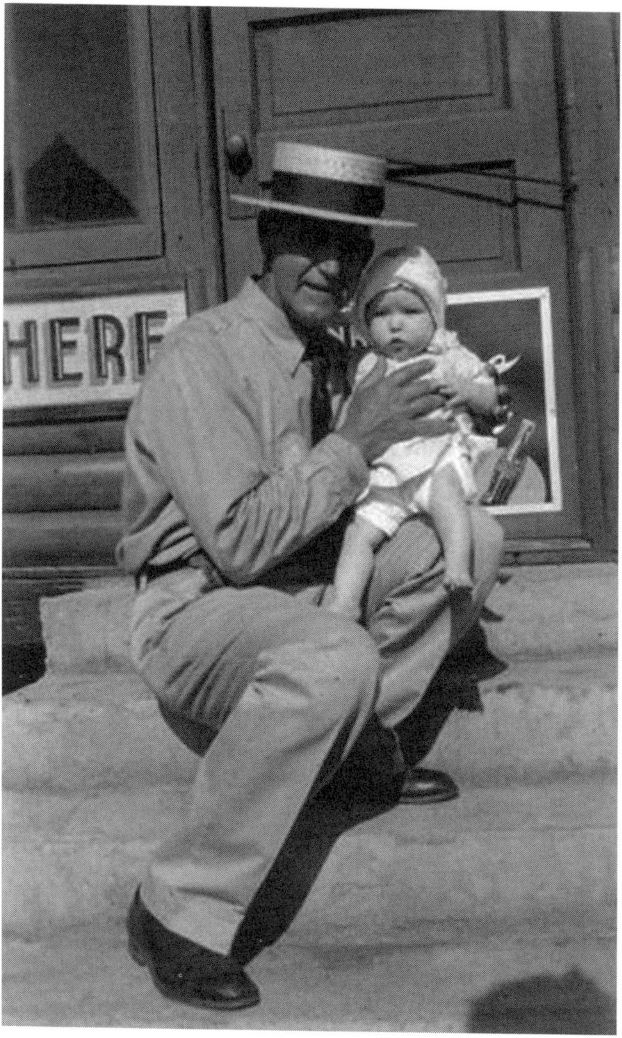
HERE

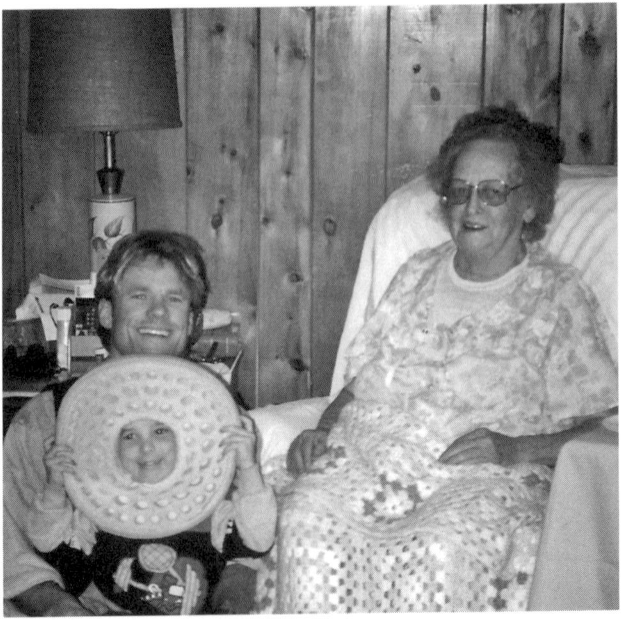

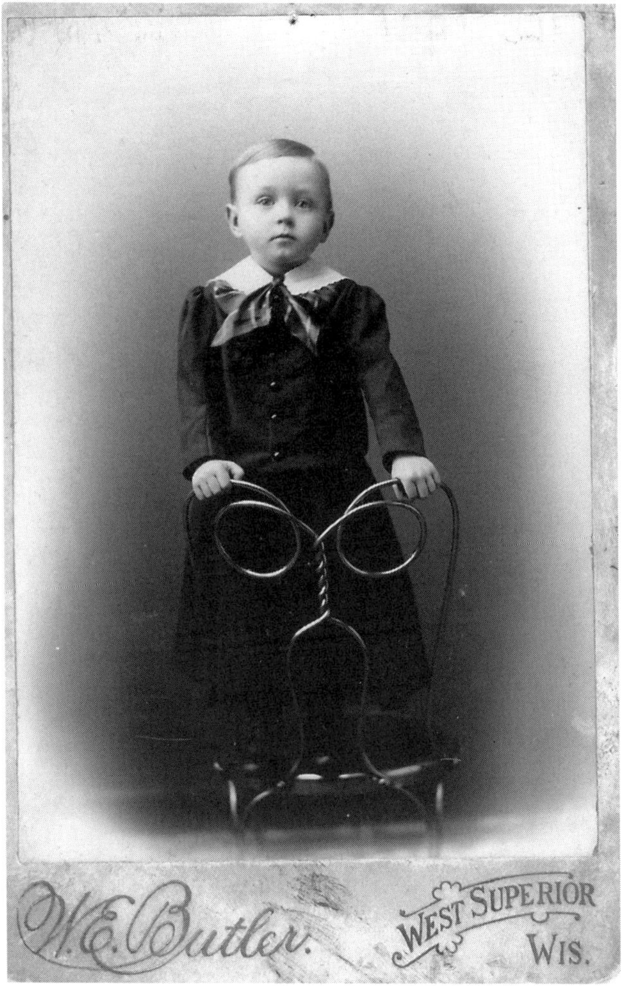
W. E. Butler.
WEST SUPERIOR
WIS.

Floss. 1910. J.

From Grandma's Pen

August 1962

Feeling that the lawn was pretty well in hand, I turned to the problem of "The Rock."

Every time I stepped out the back door or looked out the north window, there it still was, an eternal challenge to my ingenuity: a huge eyesore overgrown with brush and a complete nothing in the way of beauty.

One bright summer morning I was staring at it glumly over the rim of my coffee cup and thinking... if it weren't there, what a wonderful place it would be for a flower garden. In a flash of sheer genius it came to me: a rock garden!

I hurried out to the shed, grabbed a shovel, rake, hoe and a wrecking bar. Hmm... let's see... that should do it.

Starting at the bottom of the hill, I began ripping off great strips of sod in mad abandon. Whoops! There went a fingernail!

Back into the house for a pair of jersey gloves where my 15-year-old daughter was making breakfast for the three younger girls.

"What's the project, mom?" She asked.

"A rock garden," I exulted. "A beautiful, beautiful rock garden. On top of the rock!"

"Does dad know about it?" She inquired, referring to a

rather nasty habit he had of pleading, "Please, please don't you two dames START anything today!"

"Of course not," I replied. "He was already gone when I thought of it."

He certainly had been one way about a few little things that went wrong, like the time we tore out some paneling for a bookcase. How could we know that he'd have to hire a carpenter to finish it?

Another time, when we had shut the water off in order to line the water closet, we must have turned the wrong valve or something because the bathroom flooded and loosened the floor tile.

Little mistakes like that always seem to set him off like a rocket.

To get back to Project Rock. My daughter Sherry fell into the spirit of the thing immediately. We put the little one in her playpen, left Gail and Linda with the dishes, and set out with happy hearts to make our back yard a thing of beauty.

All went well for about an hour. We pulled out brush, tore

off sod, and carefully stockpiled the rich black dirt for future use. The rock started to slope back and we ran into flat slabs of rock under the grass and brush. These had to then be pried loose from the roots that bound them. It grew hot and our enthusiasm started to waver a bit. It became increasingly difficult to straighten our backs up. To add to our problems, it was almost impossible to stand on the vertical face of the rock.

The little girls suddenly called from the house that lunch was ready.

Oh Lordy! Noon already?!

We pulled off our mangled gloves, slowly pulled our aching backs into an upright position, and walked into complete chaos!

The kitchen was acrid with smoke. A dish towel, spotted with heaven knows what all, drooped in complete discouragement from the sink. The room looked as though a tornado with an over-active thyroid had passed through.

But the table was gaily set with all the good dishes they could find, and a bouquet of wild daisies graced the center of it all.

We sat down numbly to a feast of scorched condensed soup and charred, grease-laden grilled cheese sandwiches.

Choking it down manfully, we could only look in their happy, expectant faces and declare it delicious fare. Since they'd made lunch, we felt it only fair to clean up. In complete silence, we set to work putting things in order.

The little one woke up, was changed, fed, and put outside in her playpen.

Holy cow! Two o'clock! Where had the day gone? Well, there was enough left with last night's pot roast so we wouldn't have to waste precious time cooking, thank goodness.

With dragging feet, we went back to the scene of our crime, working in complete and desperate silence. We couldn't possibly get it done by five. Whatever would Maxwell say? Strange, I thought despairingly to myself, Max is "Max" until I back myself into a corner, and then he automatically becomes "Maxwell."

"Here's a nice little ledge we could build a little rock garden on," Sherry suddenly suggested, breaking into my doleful musing. We then began a mad parade up and down the slippery side of the rock, piling the flat slabs up from the ledge, filling it

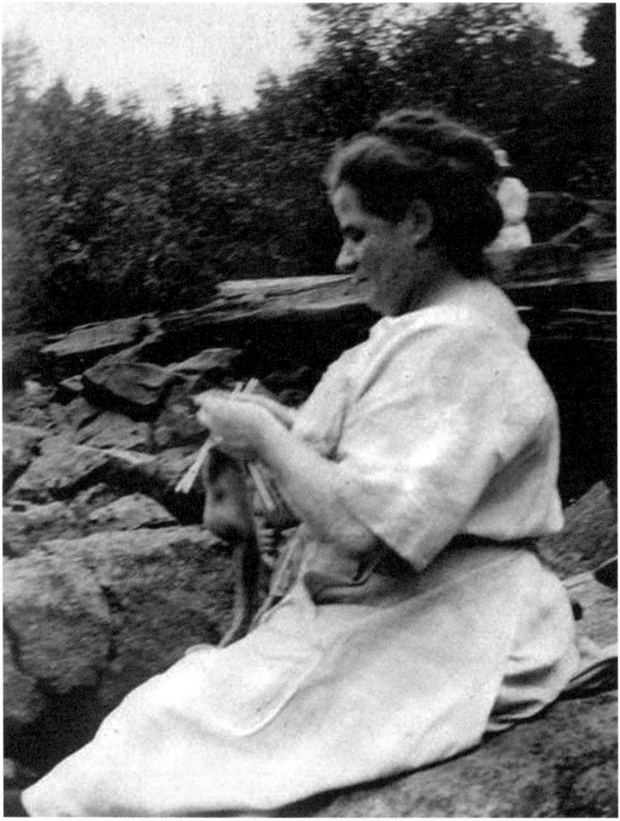

with the precious dirt, then more slabs and more dirt.

Aha! That looked pretty good! We stood below, dirty and bedraggled, gazing rapturously at our creation, which was only a fair rumor of the greater splendor to come.

The happy contemplation of our handiwork was interrupted by a cry resembling the scream of a wounded cougar.

Unwillingly, we turned as one to face a livid husband and father.

"Omigod! What are you DOING?!" (Did you ever notice how tall people seem to be when they're confused?)

Little Roz lie down in her playpen and shut her eyes as though asleep, wondering what her dad would say. Mutely I turned back to stare in marked fascination at my tender-loving spouse slowly wondering what level of intellect we must be to begin such a hideous task! He clung to the door of his battered old pickup shaking his head in that "I-can't-believe-you're-doing-this" way.

Sherry, after clearing her throat and swallowing a couple of times, found her timid little voice with which to offer, "We're making a rock garden Daddy."

Struggling to find that half laugh, Max said on his way to take a shower, "You don't have to FARM rocks, they grow wild around here!"

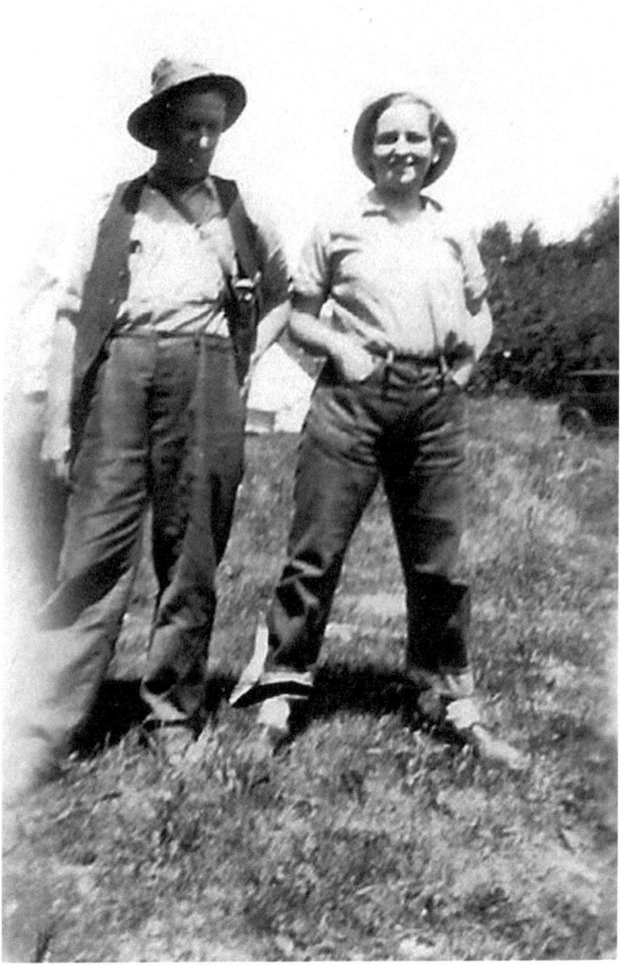

On hearing the shower run, I skipped nimbly to bed and lay with one blistered palm turned piteously upward and attempted, with closed eyes, to look careworn.

The light snapped off.

Like a mouse in a bed of dry leaves, my mind was scurrying about, trying to formulate a cunning remark that would make the light of my life laugh in spite of himself. Ah, I didn't need to do this, I knew he was happy about the rock garden. I slept.

With the first ray of light, I whipped out of bed, showered ever so briefly, whisked a toothbrush over the front four, then started throwing together a batch of blueberry waffles (guess whose favorite breakfast this was?).

A playful tug at my apron strings almost undid me. I squalled like a scalded cat, dropped the beater whisk, whirled a spattering of batter across my heaving bosom and deposited one ignominious blob on the bridge of my nose. While I did a not-so-slow turn, the big hulk laughed and laughed and then laughed some more.

The kids, hearing the uproar, came joyously whooping and clattering down the stairs. So began another day.

Max shuttled back and forth between the yard and the shed, trying not to look at "Mother's Folly." By early afternoon he had his chores done and came in to have a cool drink and read a little.

With the three older offspring gone swimming and little nubbins napping, I drearily trudged out and started on "The Project" again.

The sun was blazing, the wind had died, and a million pesky black flies were gnawing greedily at all my exposed parts. I hacked away at the crust of "Old Baldy," paused a moment to claw at a bloody lump behind my ear, and then came the great inspiration! Mr. Lazybones was going to finish it for me! He just didn't know it yet.

Stealthily, I inched down the hill with the wrecking bar, wiped off the telltale dirt from it, and stood it in its accustomed placed behind the shed door.

Now then. Step two.

Taking up the shovel, I carefully slid it down between two slabs of rock and brought the metal tip up with a grating wrench.

Silence.

Putting it back between the rocks, I pried again.

Another rasping screech.

The screen door slammed open, and the man of the house howled,

"What are you DOING?!"

"Just digging out some rocks, Sweetie," I patiently explained and gave it a little more English.

"Stop for the luvva Mike!" he howled. "You'll RUIN my good shovel. Use the bar to pry with."

"Bar?" I queried dubiously. "What bar?"

"Oh, for crying out loud!"

He stomped into the shed, got the bar (with my body heat scarcely gone from it) and brought it up the hill. He held it up and we both looked at it. Finally, he cast the "Professional Eye" over the situation and fell to work, prying out rocks, tearing out the brush, pretty much taking over. My master plan was working!

I started down the hill, and he gave me a perfectly perplexed look then asked bitingly, "And where might you be going, Madame Landscape Artist?"

"Just down to get you some gloves, Honey," I answered him.

After handing him the gloves and getting an ungrateful grunt in return, I decided a bit of buttering up would not be amiss and proceeded to slather it on forthwith. When it started to get a bit thick, I decided to let it trail off, and I trailed off with it.

Hopping briskly into the house, I closed the screen door warily. Fine! He was so engrossed in "The Project"; he didn't even notice I'd left.

"A big fat HA! HA! to you, Mr. Know-it-all," I said to myself as I scrubbed up. Then I sat the weary body down with a tall glass of iced tea.

I could see him stooped over, sweating and tugging doggedly, and my generous heart turned with pity.

"Hey, hey there! That'll never do," I chided myself.

With great strength of character I turned away and once more applied myself to the glass with its twinkling ice cubes.

To keep from impulsively rushing out to aid my hard-working mate, I got out a piece of scratch paper and pencil.

I drew a passable likeness of the rock with three small gardens marching in steps up the face. In these I busily sketched gay, gaudy little dwarf plants.

Now for the top! Oh, there was so much to choose from! Where did I put that seed catalog? My imagination busied its little self with the riot of color that would dominate that magnificent beauty out there.

I started guiltily as the screen door banged, and he came in.

"I was just trying to picture what would look best on top of the rock," I babbled. "Maybe a mixture of annuals and perennials...?"

"Annuals and perennials?! That's going to be the best darn cucumber bed in all of Northern Minnesota!"

If perchance you should pass our way, drop in. I'm the best blankety-blank pickle maker in these parts.

The Best Blankety-Blank Pickles

Dill Pickles:

1 QT. CIDER VINEGAR
3 QTS. WATER
1 CUP CANNING SALT
1/2 CUP SUGAR
1 TSP. ALUM

PACK CUKES IN JAR WITH 2 SPRIGS DILL
1 LARGE GARLIC BUD.

BRING INGREDIENTS TO BOIL AND POUR OVER CUKES.
SEAL WITH STERILE LID AND LET SIT FOR 2 WEEKS.

(Oh yeah, almost forgot: the cukes really should be grown on a rock.)

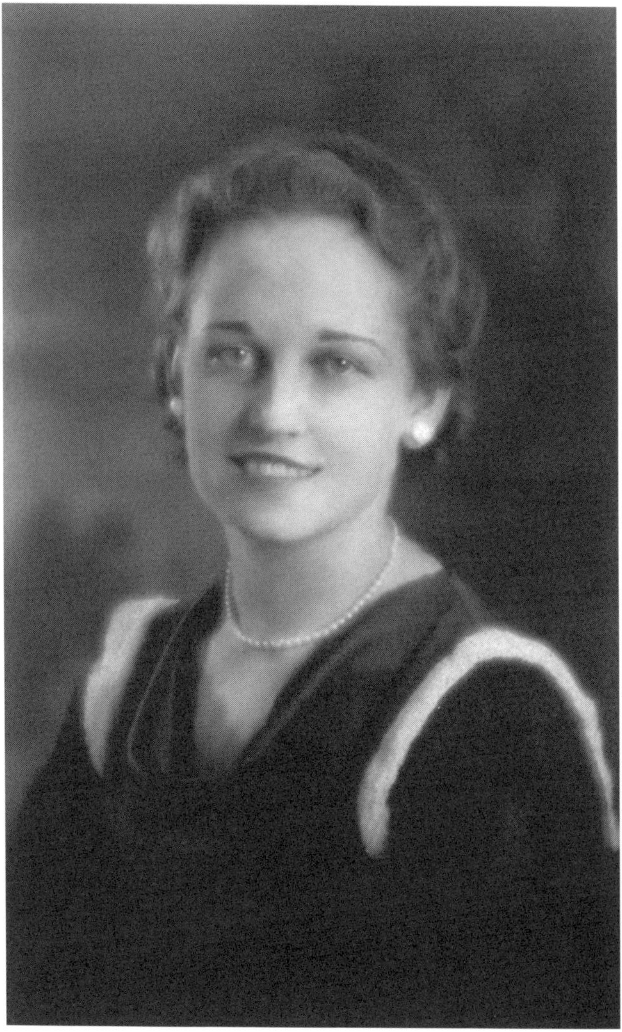

Elizabeth Lovold
1916-2006

The true blue bird of happiness.

It had been nearly three months since Mom had died. There was a cold October freeze settling into the Beaver Bay, Minnesota, air, and the snow was beginning to fall, when the phone rang at Dad's house. It was my sister Linda, and she said that if we were going to bury Mom's ashes before next spring, we better do it today. Dad and I got ourselves ready, then headed out to the Sawtooth Cemetery.

Linda and my brother-in-law Roger met us there, and we began the task of digging a hole deep enough to set the urn into. It was very slow going, and as we were taking turns at the shovel, we spotted a blue bird perched on a pole next to us. He sat there motionless, and Linda said she thought is was a beautiful statue someone had set there. It reminded her of when she was a young girl. She and Mom were down by the Beaver Bay Club when they saw a blue bird. Mom said how rare it was to see a blue bird, and it was mom's favorite bird. They watched it together until it flew away.

As Linda finished her story, the statue that had been listening along with us fluttered down to the ground near us. He flitted around on the ground, up into the tree and back down again, watching us as we laid Mom's ashes into the soil. He never left the scene all the while we were working, and remained on his vigil until after we left.

The next day Dad and I were sitting in the living room when a blue bird landed on the deck railing right in front of the big picture window. He watched us for a time and then took to flight up and away. It was absolutely amazing. As Dad and I sat there in the stillness of that moment, I found the words within me, and I said to Dad it was a sign from God that Mom was at peace and was with him.

Auntie Roz
December 2006
Beaver Bay, Minnesota

Who Are all the People in the Pictures?

Cover photo — Grandma Lizabo in her early 20s

6   Elizabeth "Grandma Lizabo" Garrison. 1936
9   Author on winter camping trip, BWCAW
10 Grandma Lizabo and daughter Sherry. 1936
13 The Beaver Bay Trading Post, which my Grandma and Grandpa ran for several years. 1942
13 Grandma Lizabo, Gail Garrison, Great Grandpa Oscar, Gary Thompson, Linda Garrison, Sherry Garrison, (lower right) Jimmy Thompson, Jimmy Wilkins, Roz Garrison. 1953
14 Linda, Roz, Gail Garrison (daughters). 1955
14 Grandma's recipe book.
17 Mason Raymond, author, Beau Raymond. Summer 2005
17 East Beaver Bay port. Early 1900s
19 Great Grandpa Oscar, Great Grandma Slater, Grandma Lizabo & Great Uncle Henry. 1919
20 Roz Garrison (top), Gary Thompson, Vickie Thompson, Jimmy Thompson (from left). 1959
20 Gail, Roz, Linda Garrison. Summer 1953
22 Great Grandma Elizabeth Slater. 1901
25 Willamenia, John and Jacob Schaaf. 1897
27 Grandpa Max. 1943
28 Gail Garrison, Martin Davis, Roz Garrison. 1961
31 Sherry, Gail, Linda, Roz Garrison). 1957
32 Herman Slater, Elizabeth Slater, baby Lena Slater, Robert Henry Slater. 1895
33 Lena, John, and Herman Slater. 1901
34 Henry Lovold (grandma's brother). 1942
36 Great Grandpa Oscar Lovold and brother Peter Lovold. 1925

37 Gail, Grandma, Sherry Garrison. 1943
37 Roz Garrison, Gary Thompson, Jimmy Thompson. 1954
39 Grandpa Max and Grandma hiking in the woods. 2003
40 Grades 1-8, Beaver Bay MN, one room school house. 1930
40 Grandpa Max's parents - Lyndsay and Marie Garrison
42 Shirley Amundson, Grandma. 1936
45 Great Great Grandma Garrison in Nova Scotia Canada. 1888
47 Grandpa Max rockin' the guitar. 1959
47 Grandpa Max playing the guitar the day of Grandma's funeral. 2006
48 Silver Creek Cliff State Road North Shore of Lake Superior. 1922
51 Grandma Lizabo. 1941
52 Baptism River on the North shore of Lake Superior at spring runoff. 1925
53 Lake Superior near Beaver Bay, MN. 1967
53 Linda, Roz, Gail Garrison. 1954
54 The Slaters and Lovolds gearing up for road trip. 1929
54 Baby Scott Davis, Gail Davis, and Roz Garrison (far right). 1958
57 Beau Raymond southern Italy. 2006
58 Great Grandma Marie and Great Grandpa Lindsey Garrison. 1958
59 Grandma in camper w/ famous hat. 2003
60 Grandpa Max w/ large walleye. 1921
60 Great Grandpa Lindsay Garrison, Max Garrison, Eddith Garrison, Marie Garrison, Sylvia Garrison. 1917
63 Grandma Lizabo's 4H group. 1906
65 Great Grandpa Oscar Lovold holding a rescued moose calf. 1920
65 Gary Thompson, Jimmy Thompson, Vickie Thompson, Roz Garrison, Two Freckles, and Flipper. 1959
66 Jacob Schaaf (far left), family and friends on a picnic. 1895

66 Slater family and friends on porch of hotel in Beaver Bay. 1908
68 Great Grandpa Oscar, Grandma Lizabo, Great Uncle Leonard Lovold, and Auntie Sherry Thompson (child). 1945
69 Great Grandpa Lindsay and Grandpa Max Garrison. 1946
70 Grandma (far right) and Garrison familiy. 1952
70 Roz Garrison, Grandpa Max, Sherry, Linda. 1951
73 Henry Lovold, Grandma Lizabo, Grandpa Max. 1945
74 Grandpa Max sporting the funky hairdo, Grandma Lizabo and my Auntie Sherry. 1945
75 Grandpa Max by grist from the old mill
75 The Slater family harvesting wood. 1904
77 Great Grandpa Oscar Lovold ready for business
78 Hank Amyotte. 1952
81 The Hotel in Beaver Bay. 1910
81 Great Grandpa Schaaf and Grandma Schaaf
82 Buck and Sherry Thompson
83 Ruth Handgartner Amyotte, Hank Amyotte
84 Great Grandma Lena, Snuffy St. Denny, Great Aunt Karen and son Charles
85 Sherry Thompson with sister Roz kissing her son Jimmy. 1950
85 Author and son, Beau Raymond, enjoying a fine pasta dinner. Milano, Italy. 2006
87 Oscar Lovold. 1954
88 Grandma Lizabo, Ole Lovold, Leonard Lovold, Henry Lovold. 1925
88 Eino Lovold, Jimmy Wilkenson, Max Garrison. 1946
89 Author and son, Beau Raymond, on the top of a Swiss Alp awaiting fresh cheese.
90 Grandma and "The Rock"

93 Great Grandma Lena Lovold. 1935
94 Great Great Grandma Slater. 1900
96 Great Grandpa Oscar Lovold in Hawaii. 1941-43 (WWII)
97 Great Grandpa Oscar with a young Sherry Garrison.
99 Great Grandpa Oscar and Sherry Thompson. 1936
98 Author, son Beau, and Grandma Lizab0. 1997
99 Great Uncle John Slater. 1903
100 Florence Slater and friend moving logs. 1910
102 Roz Garrison and Jimmy Thompson. 1957
103 Charles "Snuffy" St. Denny (Grandma's step dad)
105 Great Grandma Slater sewing socks. 1916
106 Grandma Lizabo, Great Grandma Lena, Great Uncle Henry. 1918
107 Woman's Club - Great Great Grandma Slater (in middle). early 1900's
108 Great Grandpa Robert Henry Slater and Grandma. 1957
111 The famous "Rock" garden. 1967
113 Grandma Lizabo (Elizabeth Lovold) graduation picture.
121 Grandpa Max.

Rod would like to Thank:

- First and foremost, my heartfelt thanks to my Grandma for her undying wisdom, humor and infectious smile.
- To my family, especially my mom and aunt Roz, for providing the pictures, stories, and editing.
- Simon Gray, Kai Salmela, and Teri Glembin for concept, design, and layout.
- Chris Godsey, Linda Glisson, and Catherine Long for editing.

Closing Crumbs:
GRANDPA MAX USED TO SAY: GETTING OLDER IS A FACT, GROWING OLD IS NOT.

Well into his 90s, Grandpa still NEVER talked about being old. As a matter of fact at age 92 he was still gardening, enjoying good conversation with company, missing his wife, and loving watching the songbirds. He was really excited about a fly-in fishing trip to Northern Canada with me, my step father, and some uncles. And had we gone on the trip, I'm sure he would have packed some of Grandma's raisin cake.

Rod Raymond

If you're going to be a bear, be a grizzly...
Make it happen.

Rod Raymond

Rod Raymond's other books and DVD's

Coming Soon: Quick Fit II (Fall '09)

Rod can also speak to your business or organization
(www.keynotespeakers.com or www.rodraymond.com)

www.rodraymond.com